CREATIVE INSECURITY

CREATIVE INSECURITY

LEAN INTO THE UNKNOWN AND UNLEASH YOUR INNER MISFIT

JAMES M. SWEENEY
and **RHONDA LAURITZEN**

A POST HILL PRESS BOOK
ISBN: 979-8-88845-539-5
ISBN (eBook): 979-8-88845-540-1

Creative Insecurity:
Lean Into the Unknown and Unleash Your Inner Misfit
© 2024 by James M. Sweeney and Rhonda Lauritzen
All Rights Reserved

Cover design by Conroy Accord

This is a work of nonfiction. All people, locations, events, and situations are portrayed to the best of the author's memory.

No part of this book may be reproduced, stored in a retrieval system, or transmitted by any means without the written permission of the author and publisher.

Post Hill Press
New York • Nashville
posthillpress.com

Published in the United States of America
1 2 3 4 5 6 7 8 9 10

For Diana Orrantia, who embodies the patient experience for so many others. I have had many encounters with patients in the past, but you came out of the blue at a meaningful time for me, and it felt like a God-wink.

TABLE OF CONTENTS

SECTION THREE: ASSEMBLING A COMPANY

FOREWORD

BY DEAN KAMEN

Jim Sweeney and I met many years ago and, for a number of years, our careers crossed paths frequently due to our common interest in improving healthcare. During those years, we often saw eye-to-eye on the impact that emerging technologies could and should have on the healthcare system. I agreed to read this book given this history, but then it started to feel like more of an obligation than something I looked forward to doing. I am a very slow reader and have little tolerance for the endless prattle that comes out of many business books these days.

I took a deep breath and sat down to at least skim the book. Eleven hours later I had read it straight through and found myself in strong agreement with many of the ideas in Creative Insecurity. There are so many memorable lines, and in fact, some I am sure I have said myself.

Like Jim, I am not afraid of failure. It isn't my favorite thing, but I happen to be an expert on the topic. I believe that for every step backward, you should try all the harder to take two steps forward. As long as you embrace the failure and move past it faster than most, you can get three times the experience and still end up ahead. I would rather have either a spectacular failure or a spectacular success than die in the warm death of mediocrity.

Not only did I find this book to be personally interesting because I know so many of the people and companies mentioned, but also because it has a compelling vision. Each time I reached a place where I thought, "I wouldn't necessarily agree with that," a next paragraph would follow presenting another, more nuanced facet of the argument. It gives the right examples and delivers a balanced perspective.

I wrote this foreword because I think many people will find this book insightful, especially anybody who has ever tried to start a business, or wondered whether they should start a business, and if so, when they should start a business.

Creative Insecurity will encourage people to do something that matters instead of just making small, incremental improvements. This book will light a fire for anyone with a creative side, and I especially hope newly minted business school graduates will take the time to read it.

Dean Kamen is the legendary entrepreneur best known for inventing the Segway. However, he is proudest of other world-changing breakthroughs, many in the medical field. These include the insulin pump he developed in his parents' basement in 1973, a portable dialysis machine, a robotic arm for humans, the iBOT stair-climbing wheelchair, and a revolutionary machine that provides safe drinking water to developing countries. He is an icon in Manchester, New Hampshire and he also founded the non-profit FIRST®. This 501(c)(3) charity inspires youth from all nations through a robotics sport and celebrates science, technology, engineering, and mathematics (STEM) leadership and innovation.

AUTHOR'S NOTE

Throughout my career, I started or co-founded fourteen companies with successful exits, and there have been countless other experiments along the way. There were various fundraising rounds, IPOs, mergers, and acquisitions. The company names and timelines are generally unimportant for this book, which is not a history of the healthcare industry or my business. This book isn't my autobiography either. Instead, I share the principles and traits needed for anyone to lean into creative insecurity and unleash their inner misfit. These ideas will benefit anyone who is entrepreneurially minded.

My first company started as Home Healthcare of America, but the name later changed to Caremark, which I use throughout this book for consistency. We took it public in 1982, and then sold Caremark to Baxter in 1987 for $586 million.[1] It was eventually purchased by CVS in 2004 for $24 billion.

After Caremark, I wondered if I would be "One-and-Done Sweeney," but fourteen wins have shown the repeatability of the concepts in this book. My co-author and I have

---

1 Leslie Berkman, "Executive Comes Full Circle in Deal for Lab: Acquisitions: The Former marketing director of McGaw Laboratories heads a group that is acquiring his old employer, now known as Kendall McGaw Laboratories," *Los Angeles Times*, August 1, 1990, https://www.latimes.com/archives/la-xpm-1990-08-01-fi-1609-story.html.

added the scholarly work of other researchers throughout for further evidence, analysis, and nuance.

Here are some additional highlights to give context. My team and I created Central Admixture Pharmacy Services (CAPS) in 1990. CAPS ultimately sold to B-Braun. We purchased McGaw in 1990 and took the whole thing public. This public company was sold to Key Pharmaceuticals for $600 million. CardioNet started in 2000, and Phillips eventually bought it as part of BioTelemetry in 2021 for $2.8 billion.

These are just a few examples of the successes my colleagues and I have achieved through the years. I have had the great privilege of mentoring others along their journeys, and that is why I am confident that you can replicate the principles in this book. I can't wait to see the success—as you define it—that opens for you as you put these ideas into action.

SECTION ONE

IS INSECURITY POSITIVE OR NEGATIVE?

CHAPTER 1

Embracing Humble Insecurity vs. Toxic Insecurity

A couple weeks before my sixteenth birthday, I got a job as a delivery boy at a San Diego hospital, ferrying consumables from the supply room to every part of the hospital. They weren't supposed to hire anyone younger than sixteen, but I made my case, and they made an exception. Throughout the remainder of my high school years, I worked after school and on weekends. I liked it because I am a social person, and I got to know the people who worked in the hospital. I chatted up the nurses and overheard staff conversations. I observed what was going on without calling attention to myself. I remember the smell of disinfectants and how my shoes squeaked on the floor. It was an interesting, high-energy job that kept me moving. It also gave me pocket money to buy my school clothes and go SCUBA diving in La Jolla.

But after a while, I grew uneasy by what else I saw. Hospitals were dangerous places. People picked up deadly infections, and I also witnessed mistakes. Many routine errors were preventable, caused by humans who weren't paying attention. Patients sometimes received the wrong drug, ending the life of someone who should have recovered. Then came the coverups. I heard whisperings and noticed how the hospital system protected itself, the staff, and the doctors. As a young man with an idealistic personality, this rattled me.

I saw waste too. It boggled my mind how many glass thermometers were broken. I thought, *I should invent an electronic one.* Another company beat me to it, though, and digital thermometers soon became the industry standard. Rather than feeling disappointed, the success of that invention bolstered my confidence that I had seen something other people missed. It validated my idea, and was my first taste of being a contrarian.

During that time, I was also reading the classic books on positive thinking. I devoured *The Power of Positive Thinking* by Norman Vincent Peale and latched onto his advice: "Shoot for the moon. Even if you miss, you'll land among the stars." I internalized principles from *Think and Grow Rich* by Napoleon Hill. He famously wrote, "Whatever the mind can conceive and believe, it can achieve."

At home, I would read a chapter and then go to work, repeating affirmations under my breath. Then, in the middle of my rounds, I'd stop cold in my tracks before passing by a family stricken with grief because their loved one wouldn't be coming home. Something stirred within me. I thought, *This is crazy. Hospitals are the* last *place most sick people should be. The system ought to change.*

So, as I was reading about the power of envisioning a positive future, I began to form an idea: one day, I would do something to change what was wrong with hospitals. I set my mind to it. I don't know how I knew, and maybe it created a self-fulfilling prophecy, but I remember the feeling vividly. I *knew it.*

Is there something *you* know?

If there is, I wrote this book for you.

Not everyone will see what you do. That comes with being a contrarian. My father didn't think much of my affirmations. I'm a twin, and he was fond of observing that my brother Jerry was the smart one, while I was more of a salesman type. I wasn't fond of the characterization. My brother is indeed intellectually gifted—he went to Harvard and got a PhD there. In contrast, I was drafted into the army, became a combat medic in the Vietnam era, and earned a business degree from San Diego State. But even early in life, I thought people were underestimating me. I never wanted to prove anyone else wrong, but I did want to prove myself right.

My father died in 1969 at the too-young age of fifty-six because he couldn't get kidney dialysis. He had lived putting off his dreams because he said he had responsibilities, but I suspect it was due to paralysis and fear of rejection.

Before he passed, he gave me his advice. "When the brass ring[1] comes around, you go for it."

His words meant a great deal to me; that is precisely what I intended to do. One day, I knew my chance would come.

Fast forward twenty years, and I believed it was time.

---

1 The phrase "brass ring" refers to merry-go-rounds from the nineteenth century which had a small arm that extended iron and brass rings. People leaned out to grab the rings, and if they could catch a brass ring, they received a prize. There were only one or two rings per ride, so it was not only difficult, but one also had to be lucky.

MY FIRST BIG FAILURE: IRVINE, CALIFORNIA, ON THE MCGAW LABS CAMPUS

A secretary led me down a hallway dubbed "mahogany row" because it housed the executive suites. I entered the CEO's palatial office with a huge desk, private patio, and settee area. My boss was the VP of Marketing, and he was already waiting with the president and other executives. I felt nervous and excited to make my presentation.

McGaw manufactured IV solutions, and I had taken a job there as Marketing Director following about a decade with various healthcare companies. My early experience working in a hospital had profoundly influenced the presentation I was about to give to the leadership team. My proposal had everything to do with a desire to change what I had witnessed all those years earlier.

They listened as I told them I had spent time in the top-notch Cleveland Clinic, where we provided IV solutions for patients who needed Total Parenteral Nutrition (TPN). These patients obtained all their nutrition from a feeding tube. Despite the clinic's high standard of care, these people had a terrible quality of life. They were chained to the hospital because, between feedings, they'd go home and starve for a week before returning to repeat the process. It was miserable for them, and patients had poor outcomes. Then, a lightbulb turned on for me.

"We could treat these patients at home."

It was a revolutionary idea, and I knew it could work. We could provide all the supplies for patients to administer their own IV solutions. My pitch was impassioned, but the executives shifted in their seats.

One spoke aloud what the others seemed to be thinking: "Patients could never do something so dangerous, and the hospital would never sign off on it. They'd be too afraid of getting sued."[2]

I was emphatic as I responded to their objections. Hospitals were losing money on these patients and thus stood to earn more from the arrangement. Patients would have every motivation to do it right if it meant getting their lives back. Who would be more careful than the patients themselves? Overworked and distracted hospital staff were more likely to make mistakes than patients would be. Regarding sterility, proper steps could ensure sanitary conditions, and besides, nothing at home was as scary as a hospital infection.

"This makes no sense," my boss said.

"Every part of this equation does make sense." I said while thinking, *It will work.*

As the management team dismissed me, I could see the incredulous looks on their faces. They had already rejected the idea.

Their formal answer to my proposal followed swiftly. Not only did they decline the opportunity, but they also wrapped their reply to me in a pink slip. I was not a fit for their organization.[3]

---

2 We never did get sued by any of those patients.

3 "Visionary's reward: Combine 'Simple Ideas' and Some Failures; Result: Sweet Revenge: James Sweeney Bought Back His Old Company Cheap; Never Give up, He says" Wall Street Journal, *The Wall Street Journal*: 1, A4 – via New York Public Library.

That was my first and greatest failure up to that point in my life. But it turned out to be the most freeing event too.

I had climbed the ladder quickly in every role I'd had, but I was long accustomed to feeling like a misfit in the bureaucracies where I worked. I was a square peg in a round hole within a corporate culture. Although I got along well with colleagues, they often didn't know what to make of me. I wasn't contrary on purpose, but I couldn't help but see the world differently. Despite these stifling cultures, I discovered success by following my instincts. I was too strong-willed to accept the way things had always been done, and I brought new approaches to my work, such as turning around a list of dead accounts in my first job after college.

Now untethered, I could pursue my idea. That idea became the seed for Caremark, a company that would first pioneer the high-tech home healthcare industry. It was a revolutionary concept that saved money at every level and kept patients out of hospitals.

Caremark would be my first entrepreneurial venture of more than a dozen during my career.[4] These healthcare companies collectively created billions of dollars in value for shareholders, resulting in tremendous efficiencies. But most importantly, they saved or extended patient lives in immeasurable ways.

Why am I telling you this story? Every week, I talk with entrepreneurs and rising young professionals who feel restless

4 I have experimented with many ventures. Most never got off the ground, but a few became base hits, and we had a few home runs. None have gone bankrupt.

where they are. They often tell me they feel like misfits. They see what others do not and have ideas that might change the world. It is about leaning into the positive aspects of insecurity, failing your way to success, and honing traits you already possess.

CREATIVE INSECURITY AND TOXIC INSECURITY HAVE OPPOSITE POLARITY

As my career has shifted from serial entrepreneurship to coaching others with their startups, I've studied differences between those who succeed and those who self-destruct. More than any other trait, I see people break through their barriers by embracing positive insecurity rather than succumbing to the paralyzing effects of negative insecurity.

While most people think of insecurity as bad, it is neither inherently positive nor negative. Instead, this trait has opposite polarity, with both positive and negative effects. The choice is yours to lean into creative insecurity as a powerful growth catalyst or let fear-based overcorrections become a destructive force in your life.

Let me give you an example of a time I faced down negative insecurity in my life. As a young professional, I was about as scared as most people are of public speaking, maybe more. Some sources say that the fear of public speaking is the most common phobia ahead of death, spiders, and heights. In my case, if I had to get in front of people, I would literally start to hyperventilate. One time, I was scheduled to have a conversation with Bill Graham, who was chairman of the board at Baxter. He was an attorney, had been the CEO, and had reigned over extraordinary growth for twenty years. He had built Baxter into a multibillion-dollar company, and I was about thirty levels below him in the organization. As I waited outside his office, I started breathing so fast I got lightheaded.

After that, I knew I had to conquer that demon, so I joined Toastmasters. I got written critiques of my talks and, over time, I mastered those skills until I would eventually speak in front of thousands at a time. I learned to think on my feet, and that ability led to standing ovations. I'm not saying any of that to brag, but to demonstrate that I understand negative insecurity and how to turn it into a positive. Speaking became a skill that has served me for the rest of my life

If the word "insecurity" makes you feel squeamish, you are not alone. The Oxford Dictionary definition carries negative connotations, including anxiety, a lack of confidence, and a feeling of being open to danger.

One word of the formal definition is neutral and not necessarily negative, That word is *uncertainty*. Simply put, we feel insecure when a situation or outcome is uncertain. You might just as readily feel excited about an unknown outcome as you might feel anxious.

What makes you feel insecure today, right now, as you are reading this? You might feel unsure about the future or whether your abilities will measure up to a challenge. Imposter syndrome plagues nearly everyone. You may feel like a misfit, out of place in your current environment. Perhaps you must respond to threats coming your way.

It is possible and healthy to develop creative responses to the inherent insecurity in life. You have a choice of what to do when faced with uncertainty. A positive approach is curious, open to improvisation, and ready to learn. It is an alert state of being, not a fearful one.

If you are having difficulty wrapping your head around positive insecurity, let's begin by looking for examples in your life. Can you think of a time when you felt the thrill of a new beginning? If so, you have experienced positive insecurity. The exhilaration of new love, starting a job, or kicking off a project are all times of uncertainty that bear the markers of hopeful excitement. If you enjoy exploring and delay turning back because you've got to see what is around the next curve, you know the feeling of positive insecurity. I had that same feeling when I set out to help patients receive treatment at home. Nobody was doing anything like it, so we were entering uncharted waters.

That feeling has been present in me with every new venture since. I get the biggest kick out of the early steps. Opening a new box of business cards or seeing a fresh logo on a website makes me feel like anything is possible. No matter my age, I always sense that my biggest deal is still ahead.

You may not be the thrill-seeking adventurer type, but perhaps your personality gravitates toward exploring in different ways. Are you blessed with an insatiable curiosity that causes you to pull on a thread until you untangle its mysteries? You might be driven to solve a problem in your work or to answer a call driven by the question, "What about this subject is so interesting?" Curiosity is a potent form of creative insecurity.

The discovery process is invaluable because it reveals more knowledge. While setting out for the unknown might be scary, curiosity can motivate us to push through our fears.

And if you enjoy the learning process, you already know one of life's great truths: humans are most fulfilled when we feel challenged. We all tend to expect that we will feel happy after accomplishing an ambitious goal, but the opposite is often true. There are plenty of examples which show we are more engaged when we struggle upward compared to times of ease.

I am reminded of how climber Alex Honnold described feeling after doing a 3,000-foot, free-solo ascent of El Capitan in Yosemite National Park. Afterward he said, "After achieving that life dream with El Cap, nothing is calling to me quite as much as it did. There's literally nothing else like it in the world." Honnold added, "When you know that nothing you do in the future will ever matter as much as what you've already done, it does take a little steam out of you."[5] A white-knuckle film about his ascent earned an Oscar for Best Documentary in 2018.

Author Liz Wiseman further addresses this idea in her book *Rookie Smarts: Why Learning Beats Knowing in the New Game of Work*. She explains that mastery does not bring about happiness. Instead, her research shows that people feel alive

5 Eben Harrell, "Life's Work: An Interview with Alex Honnold," *Harvard Business Review,* May–June 2021, https://hbr.org/2021/05/lifes-work-an-interview-with-alex-honnold.

when they solve problems and grow. Contentment wanes after achieving a goal.

Wiseman states, "As our challenge level goes up, our personal satisfaction also goes up." The real danger comes when you reach the top and stay there. "When we linger too long on a plateau," she says, "a little part of us starts to die."[6]

The takeaway? Don't get comfortable. An easy life will leave you emotionally dissatisfied without knowing why. Wiseman quotes the great poet, Khalil Gibran, "The lust for comfort, that stealthy thing that enters the house a guest, and then becomes a host, and then a master." That is why retirement is so dangerous. Many people become sedentary and lose the spark of being challenged. People who sink into those habits lose vitality and some even die soon after leaving their careers.

In contrast to stagnation, Wiseman describes a "fire walker" position. It is an off-balance stance, thus causing forward movement. Fire walkers are careful, but they walk very fast. "You have never heard of a fire stander," she says.[7] Fire walkers are insecure on those coals. The lesson: if you feel hot coals under your feet, then paralysis is your enemy. Keep moving.

I naturally relish new beginnings. My greatest thrills have come from creating something that didn't exist before—in other words, going from zero to one. That phrase has been in

---

6 Liz Wiseman, Live speech by Liz Wizeman at RootsTech 2017 reported in article "*Rookie Smarts*," (Evalogue.Life, https://evalogue.life/news-articles/rookie/), accessed June 7, 2024.

7 Liz Wiseman, *Rookie Smarts, Enhanced Edition, (New York: HarperCollins), 100-101, Kindle Edition.*

my mind for years, and I nodded when I saw that Peter Thiel had written a book called *Zero to One*. He is a quintessential contrarian who founded PayPal and whose cohort from that venture went on to start companies such as YouTube, LinkedIn, Facebook, and Tesla. I relate to Thiel's drive to create something new. The creative process (in the form of starting companies) has provided me with an ever-renewing source of passion. Whatever form your creative energy takes, passion will provide the fuel for your journey.

In my case, the thrill of the quest has led me to serial entrepreneurship, beginning fresh again and again. It turns out that I am not wired to grind away in one job or with one idea for an entire career. My way of serial entrepreneurship, where I repeatedly return to the startup phase, is not necessarily the right path for anyone else; it's just how I am.

The successful companies I founded years ago have changed healthcare in America, and we now have the benefit of hindsight about them. They make good case study examples. I have some great stories to share with you, although I must say that this is a departure from how I usually am. That is because I generally prefer to look forward instead of back. That is why I enjoy the company of young people, as those my age seem stuck talking about what they did thirty years ago. You stay young by continuing to reinvent yourself and by beginning new adventures.

Not all the people I learn from are in the business realm, however. One woman I am blessed to know is a hero of mine. As a young woman, she was kidnapped and held for months. After regaining her freedom, she had to claw her way back from the trauma. Her journey included a suicide attempt. But she pulled herself out, changed her name, and became a new person. Today, she is one of the strongest, most full-of-light people I have ever met. She radiates poise, joy, and kindness, and you would never guess what she's been through. She has had a successful career and is a saver of people and animals. I consider her to be a modern-day Mother Theresa—a saint. She has given herself to God. If my friend can overcome what she did, then you can flourish too.

I know you can learn to embrace insecurity and build strengths in the areas of vision, indefatigability, and humility. I am right here with you, still immersed in the creation process. The outcome of any startup is uncertain, but I work through iterations with hyper speed. Through the many startups I have personally been part of, or that I have coached through their development, you will see that the principles in this book are timeless. My teams have replicated the methods many times and validated the ideas by surveying the best empirical research of our day.

My companies move fast because I'm a cheetah. I strike fast. And if something doesn't work out, I move on to another endeavor in the spirit of "fail early, fail often." I give you this background, so you know I am in this with you. I'm still embracing insecurity and learning new concepts that challenge what I believed yesterday. I'm still taking calculated risks with new startups and relish new beginnings. I love the blank page and plan to keep turning over new ones until the day I die. It's what I do. I'm not looking in the rearview mirror because that is not my direction.

What is your natural disposition? Are you naturally adventurous or cautious? I can tell you (and data supports) that the best entrepreneurs are a mix of both.

HUMANS ARE PROGRAMMED FOR BOTH SAFETY AND EXPLORATION

You are not necessarily overreacting if you feel anxious in uncertain situations. The reason the unknown feels uncomfortable is because we are all programmed to avoid risk. You stay alive by listening to your body's warning signs that you are in peril. These internal signals get your attention, not only to physical danger, but in social situations as well. Elders have taught you to stay out of trouble and that rules are there to protect you. Your parents were not keen on seeing you hurt. You may have been pressured to abide by societal norms. Some etiquette is prudent, while other unspoken rules are meant to keep everybody in their place. Feeling like a misfit is a natural side effect of not molding yourself into other people's idea of how you should be. At this phase in your life, will you accept someone else's definitions, or accept yourself?

Let's shift now to the drawbacks of conformity. I've seen an especially fierce rule-following streak in some of the brightest minds coming out of business schools like Harvard and Stanford, and this can really keep them from living up to their full potential. It is a hard one to overcome because behaving as expected is generally helpful to them, ensuring that they climb in society. They follow a plan of success through school after being trained from birth to do all the "right" things. They go to the right schools, which sets them to become ideal citizens in the world. Once admitted, they are in the club and can write their ticket. But one disadvantage the new Harvard and Stanford MBAs face is that they have a habit of acting sure of themselves. It is hard for them to admit uncertainty. It can be a real challenge for them to take risks that upset other people's expectations. Please forgive my stereotyping here; I realize not everyone in those schools came from privilege, and not all grads from prestigious schools are conformists. I'm just making a point for effect. It doesn't mean people with this background can't succeed, and I've worked with some fabulous Ivy League people like Dick Allen, Wick Goodspeed, and Clayton Christensen who were brilliant and humble. They showed grace under pressure and innovated in their domains.

Rules themselves are neither positive nor negative; they guide normal operating circumstances. As any artist will tell you, mastering the basics means you can break form with intention. When you become comfortable with the strengths and limitations of standard conventions, you gain confidence in coloring outside the lines. To be clear, I don't mean breaking ethical rules or the law; I mean being different.

Now, let's address the flip side of our humanity—the desire to explore. Just as people have evolved to recognize the warning signs of danger, we also have been blessed with the itch to experiment. What will happen if I eat this? What else could I make from this item? What is beyond the village? Think about how many inventions have been discovered by chance, with examples ranging from penicillin to Play-Doh, to the Post-it note. Breakthroughs occur when people mess around with existing materials or make a mistake that leads to serendipity.

Here is a story from the field of medicine. In 1958, Dr. F. Mason Sones Jr. was in the basement of Cleveland Clinic performing a routine imaging test on a patient. In the 1950s, doctors regularly used contrast dye to view the valves and chambers of the heart, but they feared that injecting dye into the smaller vessels would kill a patient. On October 30, an assistant went to insert the dye into the aorta, which is a giant vessel, but the tip instead slipped into the smaller right coronary artery. Dr. Sones prepared for the worst, but thought on his feet, telling the patient to cough forcefully. This recovered the normal heart rhythm, and Sones uttered a famous line: "I've just made history." Indeed, this happy accident helped birth modern cardiac imaging, known as angiography. Over the next few years, Sones and colleagues at Cleveland Clinic developed techniques using contrast dye that shows up with an X-Ray camera. Sones later performed the technique on more than eight thousand patients, and he is known as the father of modern cardiac imaging. His technique allows cardiologists to see and fix clogged arteries in the heart, which has played a key role in saving the lives of countless people in the years since.[8]

This example shows how mistakes can introduce an element of randomness and invite inspiration that we didn't see coming. In terms of evolution, it is a great irony that, if it had

---

8 Hadley Leggett, "Oct. 30, 1958: Medical Oops Leads to First Coronary Angiogram," *WIRED, October 30, 2009,* https://www.wired.com/2009/10/1030first-coronary-angiogram/.

been up to humans to engineer the process, we would not have been smart enough to program in the mistakes. Instead, we would have crafted the rules of DNA to make perfect replicas that never err.[9] Ironically, it is the glitches that cause evolutionary leaps.

Likewise, we would avoid detours, dead ends, and failed experiments. Still, if you look back on your life, when have you learned the most? Was it when you got everything right? I doubt it very much. Mistakes advance a species.

You may prefer a well-ordered life, but a little messiness can provide you with a rich growth medium for experiments. Then, when you try something new and your plans flop, the result can often be better.

That is why humans have an insatiable desire to try new things, go new places, and experiment with new ways.

If you are feeling a restless nudge, listen to it. You might be sensing a shift and that it is time to try something new with your life's work.

One successful entrepreneur I know said she felt guilty for feeling the call of wanderlust that caused her to leave a job where she had advanced quickly to the rank of vice president. She wondered if something might be wrong with her because she couldn't just stay put and enjoy her success. But the job was no longer challenging her in the way it once had, and she felt a palpable desire to start a business. She also describes

9 Lewis Thomas, *The Medusa and the Snail, (New York: Penguin Publishing Group, 1995), Kindle Edition, 23. (Reference: Maria Popova, "In Praise of Being Wrong, Lewis Thomas on the Value of Generative Mistakes," The Marginalian, March 3, 2023,* https://www.themarginalian.org/2023/03/18/lewis-thomas-mistakes/.)

herself as an "odd duck" and often felt ill-at-ease with others who seemed to fit "what was expected" by the organization.

In contrast, her business idea was in a field where she had prepared herself, where a large customer base existed, and where she could do work uniquely suited to her strengths.

She agonized over the decision, squirreled away startup funds, and then listened to her inner voice. She knew when it was time. On the day she turned in her notice, she expected people to say, "Are you crazy for leaving all this?"

Can you guess what they said instead? "I think you're really brave."

Now, eight years later, she says it has been scary at times, but she never looked back. It was the best decision she could have made because she is so passionate, she has the no-quit gene, and she has done well. She also has the kind of freedom that would never have been possible in the confines of her previous role.

Take heart if you have ever felt wanderlust and thought something might be wrong with you. The desire to explore is as much a part of human evolution as the warning signals that urge us to stay safe.

Venturing into the unknown is positive because it will expand your knowledge. It opens you up to serendipitous results that could have never happened by sticking to the plan. Nevertheless, stepping outside your known world can be unnerving. In later chapters, I will share effective strategies for embracing your contrarian tendencies and reframing fear of the unknown into excitement for the new. The takeaway is to train yourself to see to see where misfits fit, to empower you to buck conventional wisdom. Scratch your creative itches. Stay hungry to ask, "Why are we doing it like this? Is there a better way?"

When you learn to see your uniqueness as a strength, you'll gain the confidence to spot opportunities others do not see. Sure, acknowledge the discomfort of being a misfit in a world of conformity. Just don't dwell on it. The trick is to let that discomfort motivate you to plan for risks and succeed. There are strategies for enjoying the ride and staying alive while creating something new. You can learn the habit of reframing anxiousness into positive feelings of excitement that are natural when embarking on a new adventure. This is what I mean by creative insecurity.

What we must not do is succumb to fear.

Author Elizabeth Gilbert nailed the right mindset in her book, *Big Magic: Creative Living Beyond Fear*. She writes, "Your fear will always be triggered by your creativity, because creativity asks you to enter into realms of uncertain outcome, and fear hates uncertain outcome." Then, she acknowledges her anxiety by writing a letter to fear as though she is embarking on a road trip. In the car with her on this journey are two traveling companions whose names are Creativity and Fear. She recognizes that Fear will always be present in the car and invites Fear to take its place in the family. She welcomes Fear to have a voice but never a vote. Gilbert concludes her letter with this line addressed to Fear, "But above all else, my dear old familiar friend, you are absolutely forbidden to drive."[10]

10 Elizabeth Gilbert, *Big Magic: Creative Living Beyond Fear, (Penguin Audio, 2015), Audible audiobook edition, 5 hrs., 5 min.*

THE DARK SIDE OF INSECURITY

Now, let's shift to addressing the dark side of insecurity, where fear is the root cause. Here are some behaviors I have seen in toxic leaders:

- The founder who talks over everyone and has to be the smartest person in the room
- The bright entrepreneur who could change the world but is paralyzed by indecision
- The CEO who rose too fast through the organization and developed an enormous ego to over-compensate
- The headlong risk-taker who ignores warning signs and continues without change long after doing so is appropriate

These danger zones stem from *fear* of uncertainty, not an uncertain situation, per se. Remember that insecurity is neither positive nor negative but can be characterized as having opposite polarity. That means you have a choice about how it will present in your behaviors. Just remember that fear-based responses rarely end well.

Jim Collins and his team pinpointed the role of fear in their now-famous study of *Good-to-Great* companies. Their findings highlighted the contrast between great organizations and their mediocre counterparts. "Those who built the good-to-great companies weren't motivated by fear.... They never talked in reactionary terms and never defined their strategies principally in response to what others were doing. They talked in terms of what they were trying to create and how they were trying to improve relative to an absolute standard of excellence."[11]

My observations track their findings, and I have noticed two negative reactions to fear. The first is paralysis, and the second is hubris.

Let's start with paralysis, something that hit close to home for me after seeing how my father never took his shot in life and did not want to see me have the same regret.

I have seen fear paralyze many competent leaders. While it is critical to take in data, people get into trouble when they become so mired in minutiae that they cannot zoom out to see the big picture. Worse, they see the facts but fail to accept the tradeoffs associated with various choices. Perfectionism can be a crippling disease that prevents the kind of iteration that would lead to greatness. People who let fear freeze them in place ultimately surrender their power. Doing nothing is a choice; making that choice will forfeit your destiny to outside forces.

As we will discuss in Chapter 9, being first is more important than being right. You can only be first once; you can be right later. You never start out right anyway; you become right through action. You iterate until you figure out what works. Remember, "You can't steer a parked car."[12]

---

11 Jim Collins, *Good to Great: Why Some Companies Make the Leap & Others Don't, (HarperCollins. Kindle Edition.), 160.*

12 The phrase, "You can't steer a parked car" has uncertain origin and has been quoted by several speakers. It is a line my co-author's father, Hartley Anderson, was fond of telling her and that she often repeats.

The antidote is leaning into positive insecurity. When you reframe paralyzing fear into excitement, you adopt an alert stance of readiness. With that state of mind, you can pounce when your brass ring comes around.

Now, let's address the other dark side: how fear of insecurity can manifest as hubris, an inflated ego, or narcissistic tendencies. Hubris is an insidious form of toxic insecurity. You might think arrogance stems from too much confidence, but the opposite is true. As counterintuitive as it may seem, hubris stems from *too little* confidence, or a fear of insecurity. Hubris is an overcorrection for feelings of self-doubt or unworthiness. It feeds on fear of being small or irrelevant. In short, toxic insecurity is an attempt to compensate for feelings of what is missing, not an over-abundance of self-worth.

But why is it so natural to revert to the ego? It has to do with the nature of the ego in the classical psychological sense. We are all born with an ego, which serves the essential purpose of self-preservation.[13] The ego fuels stubbornness, which can be a strength when you need to persevere. It takes a certain amount of ego to be true to your vision and shut out the naysayers who say it can't be done. Ego also helps keep us alive by triggering our fight response. We need it in some situations.

Think of it like this: if you encounter a mountain lion on a trail, survivalists will tell you to make yourself look as big as possible. That's a reasonable response to a threat in the wild. When the ego feels threatened, it can come out swing-

---

13 We will discuss where the ego has a positive role in Chapter 13: Failing your way to success.

ing. Thus, when someone with egotistical tendencies becomes fearful, they puff themselves up as a defense, or they fight back.

But puffing yourself up in a meeting to make your rivals back down is toxic. It will cause others to respond in kind or to shrink. If you want to bring out the best in others, you can't go around triggering their instincts to fight or disappear. If there is a hole in your bucket, and you try to take from others, everyone will be diminished.

Whenever I mentor a startup, seeing a founder who must be the smartest one in the room concerns me greatly. This behavior is a tragic over-compensation that seeks to make others small in order to make themselves look big. If a leader is unwilling to do the work of overcoming these tendencies, I will quickly exit the relationship. The venture is in trouble.

In contrast, confidence is believing in yourself. People who have "confident humility"[14] will graciously accept their gifts without fanfare. They feel secure with themselves. They are unafraid. They can acknowledge what they do not know and be realistic about their weaknesses. (We will further address confident humility in Chapter 11.)

The antidote to hubris is humility, which is synonymous with embracing insecurity. There has been a lot of talk in recent years about a similar idea: vulnerability. Brené Brown says, "The definition of vulnerability is uncertainty, risk, and emotional exposure. But vulnerability is not weakness but our

---

14 Adam Grant, *Think Again: (New York: Penguin Books, 2017), Kindle Edition*

most accurate measure of courage."[15] Brown's body of research on vulnerability informs our discussion of creative insecurity vs. toxic insecurity.

In summary, rather than labeling insecurity as wholly positive or negative, it can be both. Insecurity has opposite polarity; it can be beneficial or toxic depending on whether you fear it or learn to roll with it. Harmful insecurity can lead to unhealthy reactions that are related to the body's fight-or-flight response. Some flee or become stuck in analysis paralysis. Others come out swinging with a reckless disregard for facts.

On the other hand, a person who embraces humble insecurity will say, "Tell me more," when confronted with new or uncomfortable information.

The rest of this book is an entrepreneur's field guide to embracing insecurity and tapping into your contrarian superpowers.

---

15 Brené Brown, *Braving the Wilderness: The Quest for True Belonging and the Courage to Stand Alone, (New York: Random House, 2017, Kindle Edition), 154.Sir Ken Robinson, "Do Schools Kill Creativity?" TED Talks, February 2006, YouTube, video, 20:03,* https://www.youtube.com/watch?v=iG9CE55wbtY.

CHAPTER 2

Are You Restless in Bureaucracy?

After high school, I served in the army as a medic and then went to college. Following graduation, I landed a sales job at IPCO Hospital Supply, where I was given a list of dead accounts with the challenge of turning them around. These were hospitals we had alienated for whatever reason, so our company was not doing business with them. This seemed like a great opportunity because nobody had expectations, and the only direction to go was up. The approach I decided to take was one of asking questions and listening. I planned to go to each account and say, "Tell me your worst problem." Then, I would help them solve that problem.

I remember going out for cocktails one night in San Francisco with a few other salesmen, one of whom was fairly senior. I led the conversation for maybe fifteen minutes, and this salesman finally said, "Sweeney, I have no idea what you're talking about. Everything you just said is Greek to me."

It took me aback, but I didn't get defensive. I was fascinated by how this salesman saw the world. His perspective was so different that my approach was foreign to him. It made me want to understand how he did his job. I appreciated his candor, and I told him so. His point of view enlightened me.

It also raised my self-awareness that I needed to communicate in a way that was more relatable to others. His feedback helped me adjust my delivery methods. Still, I reasoned that the old way had failed these accounts, and I would plow ahead, trying a different tack. My plan worked, and within a few months, I was promoted to a product management position in New York City. This formative experience validated my hunch that being different was positive. It emboldened me.

I recently coached a young man named Lui, who is early in his career. I relayed this story to him, and he said, "Sometimes in meetings, I will speak up, and people just give me a blank look. I think, *I probably won't say much in the next meeting.*" Lui needed to hear that being different is an advantage in the long run. Trying to get along is fine, but if you want to shine, other people will probably not understand.

Do you relate? If you do, remind yourself that contrarians change the world.

SQUARE PEGS AND MISFITS

If you feel like a square peg where you are and worry that you are a misfit, consider that you may be receiving a signal. You have something to contribute that the world has never seen before. Your unique lens can help you spot an answer that others have missed.

It might be maddening for you to see changes that are needed and to get pigeonholed into a role. I get it. Being a square peg can be a lonely situation. Colleagues may look at you with puzzlement or, worse, as though you are alien. People who stand out or push against group norms can be ostracized. Others might see you as a threat like my managers perceived me before I started Caremark. You are not necessarily wrong just because the crowd doesn't see what you see.

Don't let pressure to conform stamp out your voice, or else the world will never benefit from what you have to say. Don't squelch the voice whispering that you have important work to do.

Someone who took a different path in life than most people was my longtime colleague, Teri Louden. She made a choice not to marry and have children. She lived in many places. She said, "I am probably the happiest person you'll ever meet. We live in a world of lemmings, and the people who succeed dare to be different." She was a real glass-ceiling breaker as a woman in a man's world.

Because she was unattached, she was the perfect person to help when we encountered a desperate need with a company Teri and I started called CardioNet. We had bumped into a regulatory issue and discovered that, if we located our office in Philadelphia, we would be grandfathered in under an older rule. So, Teri packed up her life and moved to Philadelphia to start our operations there. She did a marvelous job and later shared what a singular experience it was to work with the fine people she hired there. Together, she and the rest of our team brought a life-saving heart monitor to market. It was a rewarding project for all of us, and we all did well financially. Teri is still friends with people she hired there.

In our conversation for this book, Teri mused that she and I are kindred spirits in the way we have each embraced being different. She laughed in remembering that I used to ride dirt bikes and would sometimes come into the office in what she called "loud, crazy-ass motorcycle outfits," or when I'd wear tennis shoes at medical conferences. She said, "You just didn't care."

THE EDUCATION SYSTEM AND BUREAUCRACY

In thinking about the dangers of conformity, I remember one of the most-watched TED talks of all time by Sir Ken Robinson, entitled, "Do Schools Kill Creativity?" In that talk, Robinson challenges the educational system, calling out today's schools for being holdovers from the industrial revolution. That antiquated system values conformity and efficiency. When we educate people like parts on an assembly line, the system will crank out dutiful workers and rule-followers, not creators. The world needs creative thinkers. Robinson also champions the recognition of multiple types of intelligence.[1]

Dean Kamen, a friend of mine, is one of my favorite brilliant misfits. He dropped out of college and invented many medical devices and, famously, the Segway. He said, "Unusual people wrap around the ends of the bell curve. The system does not deal well with them." He adds that the system is designed to accommodate the center of the bell curve."[2]

---

1 Sir Ken Robinson, "Do Schools Kill Creativity?" TED Talks, February 2006, YouTube, video, 20:03, https://www.youtube.com/watch?v=iG9CE55wbtY.

2 David Weiss, "Dean Kamen on Education," (quoting William Lidwell, "The Dean of Engineering," *Make: Magazine. Excerpt taken from:* https://davidweiss.blogspot.com/search?q=dean+kamen).

But it isn't only our educational system that can stifle creativity. Any company or sector with strong bureaucracies will favor conformity. These include healthcare companies, hospitals, the fields of nursing, education, and government. Many good-hearted people go into noble professions like teaching and nursing because they want to help others. Then, they find that the bureaucracy saps much of their time into unrelated activities. If you are in one of these careers, you probably see what should change but not how to overcome organizational inertia. Changes occur slowly, if at all. When change does come, it generally emerges from disruptive innovation from the outside, not inside.

Clayton Christensen[3] was a Harvard Business School professor who wrote the groundbreaking book *The Innovators' Dilemma*[4] about disruptive innovation. One takeaway from the disruptive innovation model is that change is more likely to come from outside an organization than within it. The organization will likely see true innovation as either a threat or will dismiss it as irrelevant. Hence, you may never witness the desired change within your current sandbox. Because of this, you should think hard about whether you can make the difference you seek from within your organization or whether you will get further by coming at it from the outside. You may need to leave to break the bonds that restrain change.

---

3 Clayton Christensen was a good friend who I will talk about more in chapter 6.

4 Clayton M. Christensen. *The innovator's dilemma: The revolutionary book that will change the way you do business.* New York: Harper Business, 2011.

Remember that before I started Caremark, I offered the idea to McGaw, but cultural friction prevented it from going anywhere. It took a new company to overcome the notion that most medical procedures should occur in a hospital. Those entrenched ideas in healthcare ended up being good for Caremark. Nobody saw us as a threat at first. We had an innocuous beginning, but soon, we had created an entirely new healthcare sector. It was a sea change that became a billion-dollar industry within a few years because it was so obvious and so right.

PEOPLE WHO SAY, "IT CAN'T BE DONE"

Throughout the years, experts have dismissed the ideas I've had by saying, "It can't be done. It doesn't make sense." But once you do it, you won't believe how many people will say, "Why didn't I think of that?"

A similar example comes from author Madeleine L'Engle, whose classic *A Wrinkle in Time* was rejected forty times. After it finally came out and was a success, L'Engle recalled, "I was invited to quite a lot of literary bashes and was frequently approached by publishers who had rejected it. 'I wish you had sent the book to us.' I could usually respond, 'But I did.'"[5]

WHEN TO STAY AND WHEN TO LEAVE

There are good reasons and some not-so-good reasons to stay where you are. If you are learning and you feel challenged, you

5 Madelaine L'Engle, *A Circle of Quiet, (New York: Farrar, Straus, and Giroux, 1972), 138.*

might take advantage of having a salary while preparing for entrepreneurship. In Chapter 5, I discuss why I cringe when people advise new business school grads to start a business immediately. That path might be right for a select few, but most people will benefit from gaining experience and maturity. If you are growing where you are, that can be a good reason to stay put for a while.

Another good reason can be if you are using the stability of your current employment and free time to validate your idea. Likewise, some creators choose to keep a stable job that frees them to make art unfettered by the need to support themselves.

Given that you are reading this book, I'd venture to guess that you feel stifled by big bureaucracies. So, if you choose to stay, do so with the idea that you will use your talents to create something worthwhile in your off time.

WAYS TO LEVERAGE YOUR DAY JOB:

- Use your day job to support a creative habit without the pressure of needing it to make money.
- Throw your extra energy into a nonprofit whose mission lights your fire.
- Start a fulfilling side hustle while relying on your paycheck as you make mistakes and iterate. Maintaining income will lengthen your runway.
- Gain experience in an industry while watching for the right time and opportunity to start something on your own.

A FALSE SENSE OF SECURITY IN LARGE ORGANIZATIONS

I would rethink any assumption that staying where you are will afford you more long-term security. Companies are often for sale whether you realize it or not. No matter how comfortable your current position may be, anything can change. You might find it under new management next year. A change in leadership can upend what you enjoy about it. You may get unexpectedly laid off due to budget cuts, consolidation, or downsizing. Don't slog away in a bureaucracy, patiently paying your dues and hoping for recognition. Remember that companies will act in their self-interest and not yours. The only security you have is in the investments made in yourself. You get to keep your knowledge and talents no matter what.

My best advice is to find an industry you love and learn all you can about it. Build your savings so you have options, especially if things go sideways. Then, if you find your job unfulfilling, get ready to branch out on your own. When I got fired, it was the most significant opportunity of my life.

DON'T STAY WHERE YOU WILL ATROPHY

Be careful of letting your talents atrophy if your job no longer challenges you. Even if you are doing well, get out if you become branded in a role. Case in point: One of my first jobs out of college was at Arthur Young and Company (now Ernst & Young). One of the partners told me I was on the fast track, but one day, it dawned on me that if I made a partner, I would get stuck there. I would be required to do a significant buy-in. After that, I would have so much invested and be making such a high salary that I'd never leave. As soon as I realized I was about to get sucked in for life, I began seeking employment at another healthcare company that would move me closer to my dream.

We will continue the discussion of preparing yourself for entrepreneurship in Section 3.

WHAT YOU THINK OF ME IS NONE OF MY BUSINESS

You may be a contrarian, but you are still human. The more original your idea is, the more people will be leery of it. Even when you are successful, being different means you can feel alone. I felt that way throughout my time working for others.

The first time I became a boss, I realized I couldn't have the same friendships with people as before. Now they wanted something from me. I realized that clinging to those friendships would not serve me or them well. That's why people say it can be lonely at the top.

Another time I was the odd man out was after I sold Caremark and moved to the new parent company's headquarters. I soon discovered I was persona non grata within the new organization. I didn't get invited to a social event by other members of the leadership team in the months following the acquisition. Founders have a very limited shelf life in the companies that acquire them. But by that phase in my life, I was used to not fitting in.

Around that time, I developed a mindset that has worked wonders for my wellbeing:

What you think of me is none of my business.

I recently read a quote from Anthony Hopkins, who came to the same conclusion. He said, "My philosophy is: It's none of my business what people say of me and think of me. I am what I am, and I do what I do. I expect nothing and accept everything. And it makes life so much easier."[6]

Here is another example of how I turned feelings of not fitting in into motivation. After I started Caremark, I got capital from the most prestigious venture capital fund in Silicon Valley at the time: Kleiner, Perkins, Caufield, and Byers. They also funded companies like Sun Microsystems and Genentech.

I will forever be grateful for the many opportunities they gave me, but the truth is, they didn't know what to make of me at the time. The other CEOs came from the outside to run existing companies, and eighty 80 or 90 percent were Ivy League MBAs. My family had no pedigree, and my first adult job adult was in the army as a combat medic. So, I never really fit in, and they must have predicted I would be a flash in the pan. It triggered a desire in me to show them otherwise.

Early on, after Kleiner Perkins invested in my company, they invited all the CEOs of companies they had funded to a big networking event. They held it at a swanky San Francisco hotel, and the attendees were the who's who of tech startups—really sharp people. I was excited to go and meet my counterparts. We attended training during the day, and that evening, Tom Perkins got up to address the room. From behind the podium, he lifted a case of wine.

---

6 Anthony Hopkins Quotes. BrainyQuote.com, BrainyMedia Inc, 2024, https://www.brainyquote.com/quotes/anthony_hopkins_737840, accessed May 15, 2024.

He said, "This is Chateau Lafite Rothschild, and the street value is fifteen thousand dollars. Here is a list of thirty questions about people in the room and their companies. By the end of the night, whoever can answer these thirty questions will take home this case of wine. Now go and get to know each other."

Perkins issued the challenge so we would network with each other and deepen opportunities to collaborate with our peers. I resolved to take home the case of wine, and I did.

We returned a year later, and Tom Perkins got up with another case of wine. I forget now what the label was that round, but I think it was Chateau Brion. The challenge was the same, and I set my mind to win it again.

This time it was a tie. I told the other guy, "Look, let's just split this case of wine. You take six bottles, and I'll take six."

He said, "I want the whole thing."

So, I took that case home too. And you would not believe the boos from the audience because the same person had won two years in a row. But rather than taking the boos as an insult, it was music to my ears—I had proven myself right. They had underestimated me.

The point here is not that I won two cases of wine. What matters is that when I felt dismissed, it triggered a good kind of insecurity in me. I have a competitive streak and wanted to prove to myself that I could do what I set my mind to.

There is another takeaway to this story. I also knew that to win the challenge, I'd have to ask questions and listen carefully. I couldn't assume I already knew the answers. I couldn't go out there and talk about myself. Getting those CEOs to talk about themselves was not all that hard. I knew their weakness, but also, I was genuinely interested in them. I wasn't faking it. These were whip-smart people with fascinating businesses. I can learn something from everyone I meet (and not just CEOs).

Here's an example of that. A few months ago, I was waiting for my reservation at a popular restaurant when the young man I mentioned earlier, Lui, hoped to get a table with his girlfriend. None were available, so I invited them to sit with us. We had the most fascinating conversation that night and struck up a friendship. After that, I coached him in his career for a while.

The main takeaway is that if you ever feel dismissed like I have for much of my life, dig deep within yourself to find your own validation. You can achieve anything you set your mind to. Be humble and open to information. Concern yourself with being interested, not interesting. Every time someone rejects you, double down on your dreams.

Develop healthy coping strategies when facing rejection, a lack of belonging, or criticism of your ideas. Especially if you start a company that is breaking a new trail—expect naysayers to tell you why it can't be done.

I learned to cope with this in several ways. The rest of this chapter offers the best of what I know about how to be a happy contrarian.

IMPOSTER SYNDROME

After I sold Caremark, I worried that I would be "one-and-done-Sweeney." Was it blind luck? Could I do it again? It was classic imposter syndrome.

New York Times bestselling author Richard Paul Evans told a similar story about his writing. He had written an unexpected hit, *The Christmas Box.* Afterward, he became paralyzed and unable to write another book for a while. This common occurrence is called "first book syndrome" in literary circles.

Writer's block almost undid him until he had a breakthrough insight. "I suddenly realized I have no idea how to write a bestseller," Evans says. "All I know how to do is write to someone I love." He adds, "That was the best day of my life. That was the moment I became a writer. All I know how to do is write to someone I love."[7] He has repeated that formula many times, writing more than thirty-six nationally bestselling books.

Evans overcame his insecurity by channeling energy into creating new works. He did it from a place of love and authenticity, not because he was trying to anticipate what the world might want to read. That became his guiding philosophy. Evans got through his writer's block by focusing on his "why." I worked through rejection by focusing on the calling I felt in healthcare and the rush I get from creating new ventures. I believed I could do it again and wanted to prove that belief right.

7 Rhonda Lauritzen, *Richard Paul Evans Quotes from Author Training*, https://evalogue.life/Richard-paul-evans-quotes/ accessed June 16, 2024.

Let's be clear. Anyone with a healthy degree of humility will face imposter syndrome. Among the entrepreneurs I coach, imposter syndrome is one of the most pervasive issues they must overcome. People typically think of it as entirely negative, but I see positive effects. The key is turning insecurity into a motivator, channeling it into a force of growth rather than letting it diminish you. Will it propel you to improve? Will it show you how much you don't know? Will it make you want to learn more? Will you freeze in your feelings of insignificance or try to puff yourself up to look big?

Wharton professor and author Adam Grant echoed my perspective on imposter syndrome in his book *Think Again*. He says that instead of overriding those feelings, we can harness them for good. "We might be better off embracing those fears," Grant says, "because they can give us three benefits of doubt."[8]

These three "benefits of doubt" are:

1. Imposter syndrome can motivate us to work harder.
2. Imposter feelings can motivate us to work smarter, putting us in a beginner's mindset and leading us to question assumptions others have taken for granted.
3. Feeling like an imposter can make us better learners. When we have doubts, we are encouraged to seek insight from others.

---

8 Adam Grant, *Think Again: The Power of Knowing What You Don't Know, (New York: Penguin Books, 2023), 51 52.*

Of course, it's okay to feel scared. Everyone is. So, what to do about it? Research shows that trying to ignore anxiety or smothering it with happy thoughts doesn't work.

Two approaches do work. Dwelling on it can be a good strategy if you turn your concerns into preparation. Turning fear into action will channel your nervous energy. Working to avoid a negative result will give you a greater sense of control.

Another strategy that works is reframing. For example, Harvard Business School professor Alison Wood Brooks found that when nervous students said the words "I am excited" before giving a speech, their performance quality significantly increased. Trying to say, "I am calm," didn't work because that is the opposite state one should be in before going on stage. The students who labeled the emotion as excitement were rated as being 17 percent more persuasive and 15 percent more confident than those who told themselves they were calm. Similarly, anxious students who used the same trick before a math test scored 22 percent better than if they received the advice, "Try to remain calm."[9]

Other research mirrors these findings, and I see tremendous implications. We can all practice the habit of reframing our emotions in this way.

When you feel anxious about making a decision or putting your work out into the world, you can change those feelings into excitement. This draws upon your passion. Remind yourself that you are excited because you have important work to do—work that you are on this planet to do. You have some-

---

9 Adam Grant, *Think Again: The Power of Knowing What You Don't Know, (New York: Penguin Books, 2023), 215, Kindle Edition.*

thing important to give. Shift from handwringing (paralysis) into a pre-game state. Physically practice body language postures of confidence and power.[10]

You will waste your gifts if you do not find the courage to act. You are not serving the world by playing small.

YOUNG PRESIDENT'S ORGANIZATION (YPO)

Everyone needs a sense of belonging, so your wellbeing depends on finding somewhere to be yourself. One of the best actions I ever took was to join the Young Presidents Organization (YPO). It's a safe place to let your hair down with people dealing with the same issues you are. As a president, you can't take your problems and doubts to your board of directors, and you certainly can't go to your employees. Instead, you can bring concerns to colleagues at the same level and say, "I'm worried about this." "What do you think about that?"

It doesn't have to be YPO. You could also join a mastermind group of people with similar business issues or find another networking organization.

Also, remember that your friends and family are not in a position to give you the best business advice. They may fear failure on your behalf—outsized fears for the situation. They may have other self-interests or, worse, codependent neediness that will keep you from growing. Some people are afraid you will leave them behind or may feel jealous of your success. Relatives often see you as you were in the past, not as what you

10 Amy Cuddy, "Your Body Language May Shape Who You Are," TED Talks, June 2012, TED.com, video, 20:45, https://www.ted.com/talks/amy_cuddy_your_body_language_may_shape_who_you_are.

have the potential to become. They might be well-meaning and supportive but lack the business acumen to give appropriate counsel. Finally, if you lean on your friends, you run the danger of burning out your relationships. Enjoy your friends and family without venting about work. Everyone will be happier. In short, choose whom you will listen to carefully.

SECTION TWO

THE CONTRARIAN'S TRIFECTA

CHAPTER 3

A Trifecta of Traits

When I think of people who have vision, humility, and the no-quit gene, a friend of mine comes straight to mind. Dr. Toby Cosgrove was a poor student who had to work twice as hard as other people. One could certainly describe him as a misfit in academic settings. As a young adult, he began collecting rejection slips and still had them until just a few years ago. Rather than becoming despondent, he channeled those rejections into motivation. Despite his grades, Cosgrove was finally admitted into the thirteenth medical school where he applied. Rejections continued as he received job offers only to have them rescinded. (I will tell more of this story in Chapter 8.)

Cosgrove's habit of saving these reminds me of how a young Stephen King would tack up literary rejections onto the rafters of his attic bedroom. King said, "By the time I was fourteen, the nail in my wall would no longer support the weight of the rejection slips impaled upon it. I replaced the nail with a spike and went on writing." King went on to become one of the most successful authors of all time, dominating the horror category.[1] Rejection is part of the job as a writer, but most doctors are used to being the best students and doing well throughout life.

Not only did Cosgrove have tenacity, but was also willing to shake up the status quo. He says, "The enemies of innovation are powerful. One of the most insidious is an excessive reverence for tradition." He credits Cleveland Clinic for being an organization that has "a high tolerance for renegades."[2] It was an organization where the thrived, and coming from an earlier background where he had felt like a misfit helped him embrace contrarian tendencies in others. I believe his differences are one reason he became the best of the best.

As CEO, he also strengthened the organization's culture into one that did not punish failure. When I asked how he did that, he responded that it was partly by example. "As CEO, I failed transparently," he said. He publicly shared with staff when he "tried things that didn't work."[3]

I got to know him at Cleveland Clinic when we launched CardioNet, and we have remained friends ever since. While he chalks up much of his success to luck, I see this attitude as sheer humility. Surgeons are especially stereotyped as having enormous egos, and I believe his history of rejections made Toby uncommonly empathetic and humble throughout his career, despite reaching the highest echelons of one of the most prestigious fields in medicine.

---

1 Stephen King, *On Writing: A Memoir of the Craft*, (New York: Pocket Books, 2000), 29.

2 Toby Cosgrove, *The Cleveland Clinic Way, (New York: McGraw Hill Education, 2014). 86*

3 Toby Cosgrove, (Personal interview with the authors, January 24, 2024)

In summary, Toby is a model of vision, humility, and the no-quit gene—three traits that I have dubbed The Contrarian's Trifecta. Humility is the most important. This trifecta is the subject of our chapter.

INTRODUCTION TO THE CONTRARIAN'S TRIFECTA

For long-term success, bold thinkers and contrarians must learn to hold tension between three qualities: vision, humility, and the "no-quit gene."

Vision means seeing the end from the beginning. Vision is noticing where there is a burning need and where an enormous market exists.

The next trait is the no-quit gene, which is sometimes referred to as grit. This means trying several new approaches, bumping into some dead ends, and figuring out new paths.

Humility is the bedrock of the trifecta. Without it, the others will surely fail.

THE CONTRARIAN'S TRIFECTA

A TRIANGLE IS THE STRONGEST SHAPE

The Contrarian's Trifecta framework is analogous to a triangle, nature's strongest shape. A triangle does not buckle with pressure but can distribute immense weight between the three sides. Each trait reinforces strength in the others while keeping the danger zones in check.

Going a step further, the elegance of a triangle is the built-in structural balance between three points. These sides naturally hold each other in place. One weakness does not cause the structure to fail, nor does one side overextend itself or pressure the others to snap.

While triangles are the strongest shape in building structures, we see parallel concepts in other areas. For example, the architects of the United States framework of government had the same idea when they created our three branches of government with its system of checks and balances. It was a world-changing model.[4]

The balance inherent in the Trifecta is like Aristotle's golden mean. The idea behind the golden mean is that moral behavior does not occur at the extremes but is seen with a moderate approach. The best choice is to find the middle ground between two vices, one of excess and the other of deficiency.

Thus, while various principles throughout this book may seem contradictory, it is the nature of paradox to hold competing ideas in balance. The principles hold true at the same

4 Without veering into politics too much, some argue that the United States pitched out of balance when an unintended fourth branch of government sprang into existence. Agencies (massive bureaucracies) now wield vast power largely not subject to the full checks and balances written into the U.S. Constitution.

time. Merriam-Webster defines paradox as one (such as a person, situation, or action) having seemingly contradictory qualities or phases.[5] The Trifecta's traits are present in balance at once. This is a holistic philosophy where one trait in the trifecta cannot be sustained without the others. Vision, humility, and the no-quit gene must all must be present so you can draw from them in rapid succession.

When we focus on one type of problem, the triangle will shift its shape, with one side elongating. In other words, the trifecta is not necessarily an equilateral triangle. While the angles of a triangle must always equal 180 degrees, the various sides can shift in length to accommodate a change in shape while maintaining the overall strength. In the Contrarian's Trifecta, all three traits are always present, holding the others in check so the triangle does not break. When you can quickly shift from one skill to another in the Trifecta, you can solve problems fast.

AN INTRODUCTION TO VISION

In subsequent chapters, we will explore the three traits more fully, but let's briefly get a flavor now.

Vision is a critical trait for a contrarian. It is seeing what others do not. It is taking in data points and reading the landscape. It's about leveraging the creative spark to perceive possibilities and new beginnings. It is about listening intently. Part of an entrepreneur's job involves drawing from all the senses,

5 Merriam-Webster.com Dictionary, s.v. "paradox," accessed May 18, 2024, https://www.merriam-webster.com/dictionary/paradox.

including both those we can quantify and our intuitive abilities that are not wholly understood. Vision is about sensing, perceiving, and understanding.

AN INTRODUCTION TO THE NO-QUIT GENE

Sensing without action is useless. If you get overloaded by data, then you fall into analysis paralysis. On the other side of the triangle is the "no-quit gene," which I sometimes call "indefatigability." It's also labeled as "grit" in Angela Duckworth's body of work. Duckworth's TED talk on the subject is among the most viewed of all time. Her subsequent book *Grit: The Power of Passion and Perseverance* was a #1 New York Times bestseller, staying on that list for 21 weeks. Her work struck a chord, making the word "grit" one of the biggest educational policy trends in recent years.

Once you have used your visionary skills to take in data points, move forward with courageous decisiveness. This part of the Trifecta will help you persevere until you make your vision a reality. The no-quit gene is about creative problem-solving. Strategies, ideas, and even companies might change, but you never give up on yourself. You never give up on your dream of moving the needle for others. In a word, the no-quit gene is about "doing."

AN INTRODUCTION TO HUMILITY

The triangle's base is humility, the foundation upon which everything else builds (or crumbles without). Humility reminds you to be flexible in accomplishing a goal as you exercise the no-quit gene. It keeps you detached from a narrow idea of success, remaining open to new possibilities that might be even better than what you had in mind. It is about accepting reality as you set aside what you think you know or want. Humility involves listening to others without judgment or defensiveness. It allows you to lean into the unknown because you accept that the unknown exists; in other words, you don't know everything. Humility keeps you alive by allowing you to remain clear-eyed and to not succumb to magical thinking. Humility allows you to ask for help when you need it. And it will get you out of trouble when your plans go awry.

When you create a culture of humility in your organization, everything is easier. I once coached a founder who realized he had a hubris problem that started with the CEO he had hired. After removing those people who were unwilling to change, he said it felt like a different company. He observed that when you start with a culture of humility, everything else falls into place quickly.

Humility also involves service. Effort fueled by ego will ultimately fail, but humility channels work into causes that further the greater good. When your work is bigger than you, you will be even more indefatigable.

THE TRIFECTA AND OTHER LEADERSHIP MODELS

I have noticed that The Contrarian's Trifecta model is similar to but expands on what Jim Collins and his research team called "Level 5 leadership" in their book *Good to Great*. As they analyzed the traits that enabled companies to make the leap toward greatness, they were mindful of not assuming it was because of leadership. Collins kept telling the research team, "I don't like this cult of leadership thing. Let's downplay it."[6] Yet, the team pushed back because they noticed that there *was* something special about the CEOs who were in place when a company shifted toward greatness. The researchers decided they could not ignore this, that something was interesting about these leaders. They ruminated on what to call it and couldn't develop a term they felt embodied all the traits, so they just named it "Level 5" leadership.

Here are the five traits Collins and his team observed in "Level-5 leaders," with how they correspond to our Trifecta:

1. A personal sense of humility (humility)
2. A deep understanding of one's strengths and weaknesses (humility and vision)
3. A laser-like focus on the organization's purpose (vision and the no-quit gene)
4. A passionate commitment to continuous learning (vision and humility)
5. A relentless determination to do what is right, not what is easy (the no-quit gene and humility)

Collins and I both believe that a person can grow into an extraordinary leader. The quality of leadership is "far more than simply the sum of its parts." Collins goes on to describe Level-5 leaders: "They are a study in duality: modest and will-

---

6 Jim Collins, *Good to Great, (New York: Harper Business, 2001, Kindle Edition), 21.*

ful, shy, and fearless. They lead in a spirit of service, putting the needs of their team and company first."[7] That sounds like the Trifecta's balance to me!

His team's conclusions about humility also track my observations of founders who will succeed and those who will unravel. Humility is the bedrock of leadership. Similarly, I noticed that humility must balance with fierce tenacity. That is the "no-quit" side of the Trifecta.

There is one key difference between what Collins and his team studied in *Good to Great* compared to our framework here. Namely, we focus on startups and other creative endeavors, whereas the leaders in the *Good to Great* took the helm of existing companies that were already publicly traded. Those leaders turned large companies from mediocrity into ultra-high performance. While many of the same principles apply in either model, there are some personality differences between a typical startup founder and the CEO who comes in later. As an early-stage founder, I would already be out of the picture by the time a company would qualify for inclusion in the *Good to Great* study.

Thus, business phase and enterprise size may explain why there is not such a strong emphasis on vision in the *Good to Great* model, whereas vision is essential to our model. Vision is practically synonymous with entrepreneurship in most people's minds. Founders can see new ways of solving old problems. An entrepreneur especially needs *contrarian* vision to start something novel. Entrepreneurs tend to be outliers and

---

7 Collins, *Good to Great, 22.*

misfits whereas large-company CEOs must be adept at managing politics.

YOU CAN SUCCEED *FOR A WHILE* ON TWO OF THE THREE TRAITS

The Trifecta concept matters because all three traits are needed to hold the others in check. It's easy to find people who have done well on the strength of two qualities, and it is also easy to see examples of people who crash because they lacked a third. Most often, a lack of humility will undo the other two. A healthy dose of humility can generally counteract the downsides of the other two, but hubris is ultimately the great undoer. (We will discuss this in more detail in Chapters 11 and 12.)

Remember, the triangle's inherent strength focuses on checks and balances. There is a tension between all three sides. Now, let's walk through some thoughts on *how* the traits counterbalance each other.

INDEFATIGABILITY WITHOUT VISION

If you have the no-quit gene without vision, you will doggedly move forward without reevaluating *what you should* go after. If you run headlong into a new venture while ignoring signs of danger, it can be a fool's errand. But if you do have vision, you will take in data and evaluate options before going too far down a dead-end path. Once you embark, you must constantly pan the landscape so you can make course corrections. Adjusting course by small degrees will dramatically change where you land at the end of a long journey. If you correct well as you go along, you will make it home, but even slight errors can result in a trajectory that can land you miles from your target.[8] In summary, you may miss important signals and become tunnel-visioned if you have the no-quit gene without contrasting perspectives.

INDEFATIGABILITY WITHOUT HUMILITY

Indefatigability without the humility to admit a need to change is ordinary stubbornness. Having the no-quit gene is a strength unless *you are wrong*. Indefatigability gives you the impetus to act, while humility allows you to accept when you have veered off course. In Chapter 10, we will further discuss a piece of advice that acts as a counterbalance to indefatigability: "Don't marry a mistake."

Humility allows you to ask for help, admit mistakes, and benefit from the talents of others. When you are humble, you can surrender to *what is* without deluding yourself with what you *hope will be*. Real, practical issues exist in any creative endeavor.

VISION WITHOUT INDEFATIGABILITY

Many people have flashes of inspiration and can see what should change but don't have the will to make it happen. As soon as things get hard, they quit. You will never reach your potential if you have great ideas but lack follow-through. Vision without work ethic is flakiness.

---

8 James Clear, *Atomic Habits, (New York: Avery, 2018), 17.*

HUMILITY WITHOUT INDEFATIGABILITY

If you are humble and adaptable but lack conviction, you are susceptible to outside pressures and people-pleasing. Yes, you've got to listen and consider counsel, but the ultimate responsibility to make decisions rests with you. Have faith in your vision without conceding to other authority. Humility without grit will be seen as milquetoast, not standing for anything.

The good news is that you can practice each trait as a discipline. Nobody is born a genius in all three areas, and most people have at least one weakness that needs work. Our next chapter will address how to learn and practice these disciplines.

CHAPTER 4

Vision, Grit, and Humility Can Be Learned

Do you see the world differently? If yes, and if this has made you feel like a misfit in the past, it's time to change your mindset. If you gain nothing else from this book, I invite you to see your differences as superpowers.

What other strengths do you possess? Take some time to ponder and journal this question: What comes easily to you that others find challenging?

Pastor Rick Warren says, "Humility is not thinking less of your strengths; it is being honest about your weaknesses."[1] Appreciate your gifts and intentionally put yourself in an environment that plays to your strengths. Acknowledging your gifts is not hubris; it is gratitude. It is practical wisdom to realize that you will go further by enhancing your strengths than by obsessing about weaknesses. Yes, acknowledge them. Yes, mitigate them. But spend more energy on growing your talents.

1 Rick Warren, *The Purpose Driven Life: What on Earth am I Here for? (Zondervan, Audible audiobook version), 9 hrs., 38 min.*

As I have coached founders, some of the most common questions they ask is, “Can these traits be learned?” “What if I look in the mirror and don’t see a great leader looking back? Is there hope for me?” My answer is that you have the seeds of greatness, as evidenced by your natural talents and the hard work you have done to develop your strengths. All of us have areas of weakness that we must overcome. And while it would be unwise and inefficient to throw excessive energy into trying to turn your weakest points into strengths, you *can* build muscles to strengthen them until they are adequate. Systems can also help keep negative traits from running amok.

Although your weaknesses will not rival your natural superpowers, they can undermine those talents if you are not careful. People are fond of citing the brilliance of Steve Jobs, and I admire his genius as well. However, he caused unnecessary suffering to those in his wake because of his unchecked behaviors.

While a person may naturally shine in one or two areas, we all need to work on other habits. Each of the three traits can be learned. But they can also be unlearned. Once we have these skills, it’s easy to get lazy and lose our edge. Accepting the challenge again and again is to walk the path of greatness.

VISION ISN’T A TALENT; IT IS ACQUIRED

Much of an entrepreneur’s vision comes from having enough experience in an industry to intuitively sense what is coming. People might think the best entrepreneurs have a sort of clairvoyance, but this trait is more practical than that. Experience is having seen enough data points in the past to pick up on new data and triangulate what will happen. Triangulation is a geometry-based surveying term that means observing known data points and plotting where the next point will be. The same process applies in business where you can evaluate data and predict what will happen because you have seen similar situations before.

Nobody is born with that kind of experience. That is why it took until I was thirty-six to prepare for starting my first venture. Incidentally, the average age of founders who start venture-capital-backed companies is thirty-eight.[2]

Another aspect of vision is constantly panning the horizon to take in those data points. I'm naturally curious and watchful, but we all need to see more than we can with our own eyes. Create systems for collecting data, especially facts you would rather ignore. Build a culture that values questions, debate, and listening. Hearing dissent can be scary, but these habits are central to leaning into insecurity. This is another way that vision is not an inborn trait—you can acquire vision through data, and you can create systems to bring you that data.

Similarly, great companies accept current reality. They build trust so teams can analyze circumstances without blame. When a team runs into a problem, I've been known to say, "I don't care how we got in the ditch. I'm not interested in blame. I want to know how we will get out of the ditch." In Caremark, we built a culture that valued data. It was an environment of trust that grew with time.

---

2 Adam Grant, *Originals (Penguin Publishing Group. Kindle Edition), 109.*

CAN INDEFATIGABILITY BE LEARNED?

Moving on to indefatigability, some people are naturally born with a stubborn streak that makes them good at holding on when the going gets tough. Have you thought of stubbornness as a strength? It can be. If this describes you, you'll tap into it along your journey, whether entrepreneurial or creative.

On the flip side, you can mitigate your stubbornness through learned humility. We will discuss this further in Chapter 11.

But what if you're not especially stubborn or naturally good at following through? What if you haven't always been a finisher? What if procrastination and resistance have held you back? The good news is that you can learn diligence, which we will discuss in Chapter 8. Even finishing one challenging goal will change you forever. If you finish once, you'll know you are a finisher. In his excellent book, *The War of Art*, Stephen Pressfield says that the war against resistance must fought anew every day[3] but if you slay the dragon of resistance once, it will never have the same power over you.[4]

You can further compensate for your weaknesses if you embrace the third and most important trait of the trifecta: humility.

---

3 Stephen Pressfield, *The War of Art: Break Through the Blocks and Win Your Inner Creative Battles, (New York: Black Irish Entertainment LLC, 2018), 14.*

4 Stephen Pressfield, *Do the Work, (Brilliance Audio, Audible audiobook version, 2011,) 1 hr., 25 min.*

HUMILITY CREATES WILLINGNESS TO LEARN THE OTHER TRAITS

I doubt that humility comes naturally to anyone, because we're all born with an ego. The ego serves an essential purpose. Ego helps keep us alive and striving, but we must all govern it.

Also, if you struggle with the manifestations of toxic insecurity, then you will need to do some deep work on humility. Remember that toxic insecurity is an overcompensation for a lack of self-worth, not because of too much.

If you see hubris in yourself, there's no way around it: you have work to do. But the good news is that if you naturally feel the call to serve, and if it is for noble reasons, you already have the seeds of humility. You are driven by helping others. That is the seed of servant leadership, of humility, and it will temper your natural selfishness.

HUMILITY IS A LEARNED DISCIPLINE

More than the other traits, you develop humility with effort. You don't "have" humility; you practice it. People with the drive to persevere rarely possess all the natural humility to succeed long-term. However, if you practice humility habits long enough, you can grow into your potential as a leader. We all become our habits, so this is a matter of training.

Pause now and make an honest assessment of your humility. Be careful about self-delusion in this exercise. Do you naturally listen, or do you get defensive? Do you talk over others? Do you need to be perceived as smart? Are you motivated by a desire to serve? Do you possess natural empathy?

MOTIVATING QUESTIONS

Now, how much do you want to obtain or hone the traits of the trifecta? Do you want to enhance your strengths and mitigate your weaknesses? Do you want to do the work of implementing systems?

You can build the habits and systems, but you must first want to do so. How much do you want it? You must be willing to do the work. If you are willing, then rest of this book is a guide to how.

CHAPTER 5

VISION

Early after Caremark received funding from the venture fund Kleiner, Perkins, Caufield, and Byers, I attended a gathering of founders. At that meeting, Brook Byers presented me with a trophy with an inscription that read, "Jim Sweeney, Visionary." It was meaningful to me at the time and still is. Yet, there is more to the visionary title than most people realize. That trophy wasn't a talent award. Vision is largely a skill, not a talent, which means you can learn it.

When we think of traits related to entrepreneurship, vision probably tops the list. We might recall a leader who had a big idea and who led with bold risk-taking. Especially here in America, our culture has built up a mystique around entrepreneurs with vision. Controlled studies have shown that people consistently favor those who seem to have inborn gifts compared to "strivers."[1] Our culture bestows admiration upon the talented.

I suspect that when people have labeled me as a visionary, they have seen it as a natural gift, but I firmly believe other-

---

1 Angela Duckworth, *Grit: The Power of Passion and Perseverance*, (New York: Scribner, 2016), Kindle Edition, 24.

wise. Vision results from practices, habits, and mindsets more than genetics. Vision is also a function of experience in a field, and we will do a deep dive on that later in this chapter.

While it is called vision, it's not mysterious like psychic abilities. Vision stems from asking questions, collecting data, triangulating outcomes, and testing for what won't work. Experience helps us process what we see and predict where the future is going.

CONTRARIANS SEE THROUGH A DIFFERENT LENS

A contrarian is a visionary because we see the world differently than others. We say, "I think the way it's being done is suboptimal, and I can do it better." The contrarian asks, "Why are we doing it like this? Surely there is a better way. Have we ever thought about this? Can we do that?" We see what is possible, whereas other people often only see what is.

Entrepreneurs join artists and other creators with this ability. Here is an example of how one artist changed her community for the better. Kathy Peterson was a young artist living in a small farming community. Her town was economically depressed as other parts of the state flourished, and people felt ashamed of the run-down condition of Main Street. Two pioneer era buildings had become dilapidated eyesores, catching the ire of residents. City officials approved a developer's plans to demolish and replace them with a car wash.

Kathy and two of her neighbors saw the buildings as representing the town's history and believed they should be preserved. People in town thought the women were odd and began whispering behind their backs. The three women lived in a cul-de-sac, and folks began calling them the "circle sisters." It was not a flattering term. Undaunted, they joined with a few other voices to save the buildings. They were not making headway, so Kathy felt inspired to paint a watercolor—not as the buildings were—but as they could be again.[2] She took her art to show the city's economic development manager, and in that moment, he caught the vision. She had literally painted the picture. He vowed to help, and just in time. Demolition crews arrived onsite to find residents blocking their work until they could give the buildings a formal stay of execution. It sounds like an exaggeration, but newspaper articles from the day confirm what happened.

Meanwhile, the economic developer found a grant that would provide seed money. They began selling prints of Kathy's painting to raise funds, and this gave people a sense of ownership. It took time, but the community eventually restored the buildings into stunning showpieces, creating a craft co-op and event space in one, and the world-class Granary Arts center in the other. Today, the community's heritage festival takes place on the doorsteps of these buildings, drawing people from across the state each year.[3]

This story is an example of how anyone can embrace seeing the world differently. If your natural outlook is through a

---

2 Personal interview between Kathy Peterson and Rhonda Lauritzen, October 5, 2018. See also: Evalogue.Life, "The Untold history of the Ephraim Relief Society Granary," YouTube, video: 3:50, https://www.youtube.com/watch?v=Y7L1Qtjskdc&t=3s.

3 Rhonda Lauritzen, "History of the Ephraim Relief Society Granary," Granary Arts, https://www.granaryarts.org/history-of-the-ephraim-relief-society-granary, accessed June 16, 2024

contrarian lens, it may have been beaten out of you by bureaucracy, the school system, or well-meaning family members. The "circle sisters" can attest to the sting felt when people ostracize you for challenging their ideas. If the world has not appreciated your vision in the past, you'll want to get back in touch with this strength.

Vision isn't critical if you plan to work for someone else, but a successful entrepreneur must sense what's coming before other people catch hold. An entrepreneur leads by saying, "This is the way to go. We can transform this industry."

I also want to add that true visionaries not only see what should change but also *believe they can do something about it.* There is no value in pointing out what is wrong without the will to make the change.

We all know people who excel at pointing out flaws in others, mistakes made by leaders, and problems in the organization. They are contrary, that's for sure, but they are not helpful. I have little tolerance for people like this. I don't focus on blame when we identify issues, and in return, I expect everyone in the room to bring their A-game to solve them. Complainers and blamers do not last long. I want to hear bad news straight, but I have little patience for fatalistic negativity. Contrarian visionaries see the way forward and have a positive mindset to get there.

People say you are what you eat. I say you are what you think. "If you think you can or think you can't, you're probably right."[4]

---

4 This famous quote is attributed to Henry Ford.

THE MAKINGS OF VISION

In the following sections, we will explore three types of inputs to expand your vision:

- Intuition and "the call"
- Experience
- Data

VISION IN THE FORM OF A CALL

Do you have a calling or feeling of purpose that you were put on this earth to do something? Not everyone does, and often this feeling is acquired with time. Your sense of calling gives you clarity for where you are headed and passion to fuel your no-quit gene.

My call began when I was sixteen and knew I wanted to do something to help people stay out of hospitals. I realized nobody wants to be there, and most people shouldn't be. I knew there had to be a better way.

Looking back now, I can see I was set on a track then that would become my life's work. Where did that seed come from? It partly came from observation—from seeing situations in hospitals that I desperately wanted to change. But it also seemed to come from something bigger. It was a calling.

That didn't mean I started a business right away. It took me many years to gain the experience I needed. I went through a lot of preparation. I got drafted and became an army medic. I graduated from college when I was twenty-eight but didn't start my first company until eight years later, despite knowing that was what I wanted to do. Instead, I worked for healthcare companies on both the manufacturing and distribution sides. I didn't know it then, but I was meeting people who would come aboard when I started that company. Those years were terrific. Not only did I come of age in the industry, but I also built relationships.

In time, I learned more about the history of hospitals, which validated my initial impression: you shouldn't aggregate sick people so they can collectively get sicker together. That idea was reinforced by the first thing people in the hospital ask: "When can I go home?"

Hospitals were initially created for the medically indigent, while wealthy people were treated at home. We went from hospital care in the 1950s, when a stay might cost twelve dollars a day for a room, to thousands per day now. Hospitals went from the last place you go to the first place you go. When the time did come to start my own company, I had figured out a better way and was able to convince investors.

All my jobs after high school reinforced my belief that I was meant to make a difference in the healthcare field. It seems remarkable to have sensed that at the time, but I did not waver in my belief that the day would come. I don't recall sharing that notion with others. I just prepared and watched.

Occasionally, inspiration or a sense of purpose will feel like it comes from another plane. Creators talk about the "muse," giving them ideas that feel like gifts. Entrepreneurs may have the flash of an idea that becomes the seed of a business.

If you have a sense that you are meant to do a particular type of work, pay attention. That may be more than a fleeting creative idea; it may be a calling to your life's work. This type of calling becomes a kind of compass or guiding star, and it will motivate you through times of doubt. This belief is your "why." It's what you do because you must. If your call is strong enough, it will serve as the fuel of indefatigability.

Author Stephen Pressfield explains this call in his book *The Artist's Journey*, "It's as though some Cosmic Assignment Desk, with access to our test scores and aptitude charts (that we ourselves have never seen), is suddenly calling us forward and with absolute authority handing us our orders packet. The artist's journey is nothing if not full of surprises."[5]

But what if you haven't figured out your calling yet? What if you feel a tug toward entrepreneurship but haven't had the seed of an idea? What if you don't know what your work passion will be? Don't worry. As you grow in your field, clarity is likely to come. Also, if you are a spiritual person, I recommend letting God or the Universe know you are available and ready to serve. Send in your papers.

When you are ready, the call will come. Finding your passion might take years and catch you by surprise, but when it comes, you will know. For a practical roadmap for discovering your interest, Angela Duckworth's work on Grit provides helpful insights related to this topic, which we will further discuss in Chapter 14.

---

5 Steven Pressfield, *The Artist's Journey, (New York: Black Irish Entertainment LLC, 2018), 114.*

If you have already felt the call, ask what might be holding you back. Timing can be a good reason. Maybe you need to arrange your finances, test the market, or build the foundation while you still have employment. These activities can legitimately take a while. Don't do anything dumb, like taking a flying leap off a building. (We will talk more about *calculated* risks in Chapter 10). If you have felt a call but it's still too nebulous to be actionable, then take steps in that direction, and be on the lookout for the right opportunity.

Once you have vetted your idea and feel prepared, don't let fear of the unknown or worries about criticism keep you from making a leap of faith. If you know it is time but do not act, a sense of unrealized potential will eat you alive.

VISION COMES FROM EXPERIENCE

The second source of vision is practical. It comes from both maturity and experience in your industry. There was no shortcut to the insights I gained before starting Caremark. I had heard the call much earlier, but I wasn't ready yet.

It scares me when I see kids graduating from college who believe they are ready to start their own company straightaway. Professors who never did it are encouraging them to write business plans and take the leap, but I think that's wrong, and I have had spirited disagreements with some of these professors.

I held this contrarian opinion and shook my head when I watched Elizabeth Holmes and her meteoric rise to stardom when she founded Theranos, a company that claimed they could perform eight hundred medical tests on a single drop of blood. I'm not the world's expert on the technologies Theranos purported to have, but I was a lab tech in the army, among other things, and I have been around medical science for a while. My gut reaction when I heard Elizabeth Holmes's spiel was that it was a pipe dream. It is impossible to get both venous and capillary blood through the finger, and you need both types to perform the tests she claimed they could do with a single drop.

Others were more impressed. She landed front-cover accolades and a multibillion-dollar valuation for Theranos before the now-infamous sham came to light. The *Wall Street Journal*'s investigative reporting broke a story[6] that the company didn't have the underlying technology Theranos claimed. Instead, they falsified data and even went so far as to give patients frightening (and inaccurate) results when they submitted blood samples during a Walgreens rollout. Then, Theranos vastly overinflated revenue and projections to prop up the valuation. Instead of building a board with experience in biotech, they assembled government luminaries. They hired Chiat Day, the advertising agency famous for Apple's iconic advertisements of the 1980s on an eleven-million dollar retainer.[7] The whole setup reeked of ignorance, hubris, and a

---

6 John Carreyrou, "Hot Startup Theranos Has Struggled With Its Blood-Test Technology," Wall Street Journal, October 15, 2015, https://www.wsj.com/articles/theranos-has-struggled-with-blood-tests-1444881901, accessed June 20, 2024.

7 Marc Iskowitz, "What the Elizabeth Holmes verdict could mean for marketing." (*Medical Marketing and Media, January 7, 2022* https://www.mmm-online.com/home/channel/7-day-supply/what-the-elizabeth-holmes-verdict-could-mean-for-marketing/), Accessed June 20, 2024

sleight of hand intended to misdirect people's attention from asking questions.[8]

Holmes's hubris was evident, and whenever someone challenged her, she fired and sued them for breaching their non-disclose agreements—ironic considering they didn't even have the technology Theranos was claiming to protect. She gave the razzle-dazzle to investors who had little industry knowledge, because her bit didn't hold up to scrutiny by real scientists. *Wall Street Journal* reporter John Carreyrou eventually uncovered the fraud. He described Holmes's technology explanations as sounding like "the words of a high school chemistry student, not a sophisticated laboratory scientist."[9]

I suspect Holmes may have been earnest in her belief that Theranos would develop the technology one day, but in her naïve arrogance, she didn't know better. She didn't know what she didn't know. If she had been around the industry a while, she would have. Undeterred by a lack of evidence, their team probably hoped reality would catch up with the dream. They put together big names to make everything look credible. But Holmes took people's money based on a lie and because of her hubris. She couldn't back up her claims, and she didn't know enough to see why it wouldn't work.

That fiasco bilked hundreds of millions from investors and sent her to jail. She was ordered to pay $452 million to the fraud victims.

---

8 John Carreyrou, *Bad Blood (New York: Knopf, 2018), p. 224.*

9 Hsieh Nien-hê, Christina R. Wing, Emilie Fournier, and Anna Resman. "Theranos: Who Has Blood on Their Hands? (A)." Harvard Business School Case 619-039, February 2019. (Revised February 2020.)

Theranos was an extreme cautionary example, but I have seen a similar pattern of hubris from other recently minted MBAs. A little knowledge is a dangerous thing. The Dunning-Kruger effect states, in essence, that "those who can't...don't know they can't." When people lack competence, they are often brimming with overconfidence.[10]

In one study, people who rated their skills the best, thinking they had done better than 62 percent of their peers on a test, only outperformed 12 percent of them. It gets worse; not only did they overestimate their abilities, but the more they thought they knew, the less interested they were in learning. In other words, a lack of skill can leave us blind to our shortcomings. As one of the study's authors said, "The first rule of the Dunning-Kruger club is you don't know you're a member of the Dunning-Kruger club."

The real kicker is that the time we are most susceptible to overconfidence is when we progress from novice to amateur. As I see it, recent MBA grads are novices with the curse of overconfidence. The same effect is seen in hospitals, which might account for one of the reasons mortality rates jump in July when new residents take over. It's not that they lack skill; it's that they overestimate their abilities and make mistakes that those with more experience have learned to avoid.[11]

I have just seen too many wunderkind entrepreneurs crash and burn. You need some years of experience under your belt. I don't know the magic number. Is it five years? Ten? Current research says it takes 10,000 hours of hard practice to become

10 Adam. Grant, *Think Again, (Penguin Publishing Group. Kindle Edition), 38.*

11 Adam Grant, *Think Again*, 38-45.

an expert in something.[12] But it is almost certainly not just graduating from college and starting a company.

You might be thinking about other young entrepreneurs who dropped out of college and founded huge companies. Our culture has built up the lore around Bill Gates and Steve Jobs dropping out of school and going for broke. But Gates had already amassed his 10,000 hours of experience by then. He waited an entire year to leave college after developing his new software, and even then, he didn't drop out entirely but was granted a leave of absence by the school instead. Then, his parents bankrolled him. "Far from being one of the world's greatest risk takers," Entrepreneur Rick Smith says, "Bill Gates might more accurately be thought of as one of the world's great risk mitigators."[13]

And Jobs? He was initially fired from his own company because he wasn't ready to lead. When he returned, he had seasoned and would take Apple to new heights. (However, even then, his ego still got him into trouble.)

I think it is foolhardy to jump headlong into entrepreneurship before gaining some business acumen and experience in your industry. When you know an industry well, you can spot opportunities, see the big picture, and know where the potholes are. You won't burn resources on a foundational learning curve, and you won't chase ideas with fatal flaws that

---

12 Malcom Gladwell, "Complexity and the Ten-Thousand-Hour Rule," (*The New Yorker)* https://www.newyorker.com/sports/sporting-scene/complexity-and-the-ten-thousand-hour-rule, accessed June 20, 2024

13 Grant, *Originals, 20. (Author's original source: Rick Smith, The Leap: How 3 Simple Changes Can Propel your Career from Good to Great, [New York: Penguin, 2009]).*

would be obvious to a more seasoned veteran. You don't want to rush your gestation period.

Another cautionary illustration related to experience is how Warren Buffet teamed up with Jeff Bezos of Amazon and Jamie Dimon from JP Morgan Chase to make breakthroughs in healthcare. They formed a venture called Haven to much fanfare but ultimately closed it. With all the resources and brainpower of that group, why couldn't they make it work?

My colleague Bill Long nailed it when he said, "It's really hard to be successful in healthcare unless you literally have worked in an environment with patients and caregivers, and you understand the variability of care."[14]

In other words, they lacked patient experience. They didn't know what they didn't know. Bill went on to observe how standardized products differ from healthcare. "Product is something you make that is used in a generally predictable manner." He went on, "A product has expected results, but *care* is unique to the patient and the situation."

I was an army medic, which gave me experience caring for patients in a variable environment. Because of my hands-on background, I knew that when you have seen one patient, you have seen…one patient.

I could also see what would make a product viable and where the issues would be. Healthcare is a complex system because of variability in the human body and how the regulatory environment involving insurance and hospital bureaucracies function.

---

14 Bill Long. Personal interview with authors, October 6, 2022

Tech companies think they can fix healthcare with mindsets that work in creating tech products. They have come from an environment where they are accustomed to predictable outcomes. They utilize computational thinking to identify clear, step-by-step solutions. Healthcare is at the other end of the spectrum in how variable and unpredictable it is.

The point of this discussion is not how to solve healthcare issues; it's to show that vision comes from experience. That's what tech experts lack when they think they can solve problems in a variable environment with the same tools that work in a closed system. Buffet, Bezos, and Dimon were no dummies, but they overestimated their abilities outside their areas of expertise.

Before we close this section on experience, I will offer one counterpoint to my advice to wait until you have some maturity. Namely, if you feel a burning desire to start a business soon, you might have less to lose when you are young and unencumbered. You will probably make more mistakes but will earn experience in the trenches. If you are committed to failing your way to success, this is a fine path to take. If you have identified a need in the marketplace and see something needed that doesn't exist, then go for it. There is no one correct way. You are the only person entitled to inspiration for your life, so trust your inner voice to know when it is time.

VISION COMES FROM DATA

This section will address ways to set up systems that ensure you hear what you need to hear. Why? Because if you want to see strategic opportunities that other people miss, take in a lot of data from many sources.

You will only get the necessary information when you *want* to know the truth. Desiring to see clearly is at the heart of leaning into insecurity. Truth-seeking is a core value of those with exceptional humility. This means getting comfortable uncovering data that contradicts your hopes. Most people find contrary information so disconcerting that they avoid it, falling victim to confirmation bias. They only consume media that supports their beliefs. This is limiting and dangerous to your business.

Remember, admitting what you don't know is not weakness; it creates a position of strength so you *can* know. Would you rather feel strong but be ignorant or feel insecure as you build a position of real strength? It's a paradox that when you learn to embrace the insecurity that comes with receiving negative reports, you place yourself in a *more powerful* position. Accepting feedback might make you *feel* vulnerable, but resisting knowledge weakens your position because you *are* vulnerable to what you don't see coming. On the other hand, opening your eyes to blind spots makes you stronger. We shouldn't be afraid of data; we should fear not having it. What should scare us is what lurks in the dark and bites us out of nowhere.

And don't forget that what you learn might be better than expected. Sometimes you get great news or spot other opportunities.

One extreme case study is a contrast of two contemporaneous leaders with very different approaches to data: Winston Churchill and Adolf Hitler during World War II. Both were charismatic leaders, but Churchill recognized his strong personality might prevent him from receiving unfiltered reports. He acknowledged that his charisma could be a liability. To mitigate this liability, Churchill set up a special ministry outside the regular chain of command to bring him the facts.[15] Then, he often presented an unvarnished picture to the British public. His approach was to help his country prepare for deep and lengthy sacrifices so they might endure without losing faith.[16]

Hitler's regime had a polar-opposite attitude toward data. While Churchill valued unfiltered information, Hitler's regime was known for feeding the people carefully curated propaganda that exaggerated wins and downplayed losses.[17] Current research shows that this approach is more likely to backfire with people who will then become mistrustful.[18]

Hitler himself infamously only wanted to hear good news. One of his longtime friends, Magda Goebbels, was married to the propaganda minister. Her husband was the man who stage-managed Hitler's events and spun the tales for the public. Mrs. Goebbels was known as the First Lady of the Third Reich. Eventually, even she became disillusioned, and during

---

15 Jim Collins. *Good to Great*, (HarperCollins. Kindle Edition), 73.

16 Jim Collins, *How the Mighty Fall*, (JimCollins.com: Audible audiobook edition, 2009), 4 hrs., 41 min.

17 Roger Moorhouse, *Berlin at War* (New York: Basic Books, Kindle Edition 2010), 51.

18 Adam Grant. *Think Again* (Penguin Publishing Group: Kindle Edition, 2009), 116-117.

a gathering with friends listening to a speech by Hitler, she reportedly switched off the radio and said, "My God, what a lot of rubbish."[19] In 1944, she also reportedly said of Hitler, "He no longer listens to voices of reason. Those who tell him what he wants to hear are the only ones he believes."[20]

By mid-1944, it was becoming clear to many in Hitler's inner circle that the war was lost, and they should retreat to save lives. For example, architect Albert Speer was a trusted advisor who braved bringing bad news to Hitler, insisting that they should plan an orderly withdrawal. Hitler snapped back, "then the nation will also perish." Hitler then ordered a scorched-earth policy; Germany was to be totally destroyed, blown up, or burned.[21] In the war's final weeks, his generals planned to confront him in his bunker and organize their plans for surrender. Doing so might have spared three hundred thousand people who were killed, wounded, or went missing in the Battle of Berlin alone. That doesn't count the front-line fighting in other regions or the campaigns leading up to Berlin. Yet, when they met, Hitler wouldn't hear his generals. Instead, his overwhelming charisma convinced them to hang on and gamble the lives of their men. Although Hitler was in a sickly and half-deranged state by then, he rallied enough energy to spin tales of prophesies and miracles that would save

---

19 Hans-Otto Meissner, *Magda Goebbels. The First Lady of the Third Reich.* (New York: The Dial Press, 1978, rev. 1980), 219.

20 Hans-Otto Meissner, *Magda Goebbels: The First Lady of the Third Reich.* (New York: The Dial Press, 1978, rev. 1980), 222.

21 Cornelius Ryan, *The Last Battle (Simon and Schuster, 1966, Edition quoted is by Pocket Books New York, 1967), 160.*

their cause. The generals changed course, fell in line, and sacrificed their troops.[22]

Their miracle did not come. The tragedy cost not only military casualties; Berlin was left virtually undefended.[23] It was a city of women and children who had no real evacuation plan. They were left largely on their own when hordes of Russian soldiers overtook the city. The trauma was horrific.

This example is a grim reminder of the cost of only hearing what you want to hear or towing the line when leaders are delusional. It should give any nation pause when those in charge only value propaganda.

Great companies are like Churchill in that they are willing to face facts while never losing hope. The book *Good to Great* coined "The Stockdale Paradox" after Admiral Jim Stockdale. He was the highest-ranking US officer in the cruel prisoner-of-war camp called the "Hanoi Hilton" in Vietnam. When he reflected on the experience, he said the people who did not survive were the optimists who repeatedly set unrealistic timetables for release. "We will be out by Christmas," they'd say. Then, it would be Easter, and that pattern would continue. When reality dashed their hopes one too many times, they died of a broken heart.[24]

In contrast, he displayed a different type of hope. He opened his eyes to the terrible conditions they faced and then created outlets to help his men cope no matter how long they

---

22 Cornelius Ryan, *The Last Battle (Simon and Schuster, 1966, Edition quoted is by Pocket Books New York, 1967), 259-265.*

23 Roger Moorhouse, *Berlin at War*. (Basic Books. Kindle Edition), 362.

24 Jim Collins. *Good to Great, (HarperCollins: Kindle Edition), 83.*

might be there. He never lost faith that they would eventually survive, even as he understood their dire situation. He and his men endured torture and unspeakable deprivations while keeping hope that they would return home one day. That is the Stockdale paradox: confronting the brutal facts while never losing hope of eventual triumph.

CREATING SYSTEMS FOR DATA

Churchill set up a new department called the Statistical Office to bring him daily, unfiltered war reports. The book *Great by Choice* offers more examples. Researchers studied companies that thrive in uncertain times, and one commonality was that they made sure they received bad news. They were also known for running scenarios of doom in a practice the authors called "productive paranoia."[25] What systems could you set up for your business and life? Who can you trust to bring the facts?

One practice I use is one called a "premortem."[26] A premortem is a process by which you examine potential causes of death for a startup or a project early in the process. If you have a team, go around the room and have each person say, "This project failed because...." Then, each person lists the top potential causes of death.

The point is not to let people smugly say, "I told you so," if a project or risk ends up failing later. The point is to get

25 Jim Collins and Morten T. Hansen, *Great by Choice: 5 Good to Great, (HarperCollins. Kindle Edition), 36.*

26 Gary Klein, *Performing a Premortem, (Harvard Business Review), September 2007.*

ahead of potential problems. By identifying possible causes of death, you can avoid them.

This exercise helps infuse a team with humility by examining the hurdles ahead. It allows the team to speak about concerns they might have hesitated to voice before. It gives everyone the benefit of vision to understand what they might be missing. When you empower others to share their concerns, it helps everyone see the pitfalls. Then you can work together to avoid them. The purpose is to identify as many risks as possible—especially the fatal ones—to determine how to mitigate them.

Another best practice of great companies is to set up advisory groups that run outside formal organizational charts to serve this purpose.[27] That is like what Churchill did. Likewise, authors seek feedback from professional editors who are not their friends. Some people even set up advisory councils for their lives.

It is a rare leader who does this. The most common modus operandi of CEOs is to only hear from people who share their beliefs, but research shows that outcomes do not improve until those leaders seek conflicting points of view.[28] In your own life, if you have charisma, you can recognize it as both an asset and an Achilles heel. You can compensate for this by following Churchill's example. Set up systems for information to make it through to you without getting angry or defensive.

---

27 Jim Collins. *Good to Great: 1, (HarperCollins. Kindle Edition.), 114.*

28 Grant, *Think Again:* (New York: Penguin Books, 2017), Kindle Edition, 85-86

One example of how I did this was to hire people like Larry Watts. He came with me on eight startups, and part of the reason he was so valuable was that he was such a great counterpoint to me. I would say, "We want to go left," and he'd say, "I think it should be right," and then we would debate it. We usually concluded that neither of us were right, but that we should go somewhere in the middle. Larry is an affable person, and everyone loves him, but in many ways, he was a contrarian to the contrarian (me). And so, I just kept bringing him along with each new company.

One crucial way to get data is to ask thoughtful questions and listen intently to the answers. Asking questions conveys humility to others, triggers the thinking brain, and sparks curiosity. It shows openness.

Here's a sampling of my favorite questions:

- What are the reasons we shouldn't do this?
- What are the bottlenecks?
- Why are we doing it this way?
- Is there a better way?
- Why did you choose that as a priority?
- What do I need to know?
- What is your perspective?
- What am I missing?
- What are ways your business or project might fail?
- Tell me more....

If you make an honest assessment and realize you are prone to pride and hubris (and who isn't?), these systems are even more critical. Implementing systems to bring unfiltered facts is one of the best ways to practice humility.

INTUITION IS ANOTHER FORM OF VISION

Finally, as you scan for data, do not ignore the data points from within. Some have said that "Intuition is knowing without knowing why."[29] The best police officers possess a sixth sense of what will happen. They listen to their instincts. Their "Spidey-sense" is not unlike the intuition of an entrepreneur.

If you are in a leadership position, don't just rely on empirical data and opinions of others. Listen to your inner voice. Your instincts are a form of data. Decide in your stomach. I call this "making decisions with head and heart."

Let me illustrate with an example set by someone I greatly respect. I mentioned earlier that Kleiner Perkins invested in Caremark. Before they made their decision, I told them I planned to move from Newport Beach, California, to Cleveland, Ohio, so I'd be near our flagship hospital. Toward the end of our time together, Tom Perkins took me aside and gave me his assessment. Keep in mind here that Tom Perkins was a brilliant guy. He served on the Hewlett-Packard board, earned an MBA from Harvard, and was a successful engineer. He said to me, "Sweeney, I'm going to invest in your com-

29 Joel Pearson, *The Intuition Toolkit: The New Science of Knowing What Without Knowing Why. Guy Claxton,* "Investigating human intuition: Knowing without knowing why," British Psychological Society, May 18, 1988.

pany. I don't know anything what you're telling us. But I *do* understand somebody who is willing to move from Newport Beach to Cleveland."

He had processed all the data in his head and then decided with his stomach. He was betting his emotions were on point—that somebody willing to move to Cleveland would be successful. (They ended up getting 144 times their investment back, so it turned out okay for them.)

You can be as intellectually smart as Tom Perkins was, but remember, he was also smart enough to listen to his stomach. He could process the numbers and ask himself, "How do I feel about it?" People sometimes say, "I want to sleep on this." It means they want to turn it over in their mind and see how it sits with them after their initial emotions have cooled.

Intuition may seem like an innate gift, but you can cultivate it or lessen your receptivity by suppressing it. Paying attention to your inner wisdom will foster its growth. Ignoring it will cause it to wither. You can learn to trust your instincts and rely on your gut. You'll get better at it when you pay attention. Log the outcomes of what happens when you listen to that inner voice and when you don't.

It might sound like I rely on emotion, but I want to clarify that it isn't really emotion. Instincts can signal that your decision will be best for the company. In contrast, my personal feelings might say something else entirely. You might feel overwhelmed, anticipating the fallout from a decision or how others might take it. You might have a visceral response because you don't like what you learn. Refrain from letting these factors muddy what was clear to you before. I have learned to keep my feelings out of the equation and move forward with intellectually honest rigor.

There are practical limitations to intuition, however, which is where experience and data come in. Your intuition will improve with experience in your field. Once you become an expert, you will sense what others miss without realizing why.

Malcom Gladwell's book *Blink* discusses why humans are so good at taking in myriad data points and making split-second observations. It's a process called "thin-slicing." He cites an example of an antiquity expert who took one look at what was supposed to be an ancient sculpture. A world-renowned museum had already purchased it, but the expert's first impression was the word "fresh." That is not how a sculpture should look after being unearthed after centuries underground. Somehow, he instinctively knew it was a fake when it had fooled other experts.[30] Gladwell's book also discusses limitations to intuition and where overconfidence can go awry, or when we make split judgements for prejudicial reasons.

Do you have a strong intuitive sense? If so, sharpen it. This skill will serve you well. Also, pay attention to those times your gut has been wrong and learn accordingly.

I will add here that I have occasionally had things happen that current science cannot explain. Here is an example related to my brother Jerry and the connection between twins. My brother lives in Boston, and I was living in San Diego at the time. I flew to New York City and had not mentioned my

30 Malcolm Gladwell, *Blink: The Power of Thinking Without Thinking*, (New York: Little, Brown and Company, 2005, Kindle Edition) 5-6.

trip to Jerry. I decided to visit the Statue of Liberty for the first time. So, I got in line, turned around, and there was my brother. It was, like, not a surprise. I just said, "Oh, hi, Jerry. How are you doing?" And he said, "Hi, Jimmy; good to see you here." Imagine us both being in New York City at the same time, then deciding to go to the same place on the same day and to be in line just ten people apart. What are the odds of that happening?

Intuition can also come as a flash idea that seemingly appears out of nowhere. It might be a product idea, an answer to a question you've been noodling on, or a sense that there is something you need to do. When you receive a gift like this, test it for validity and then act on it.

CHAPTER 6

"WHAT AM I MISSING?"

I want to open this chapter with a story told by my colleague, Larry Watts, who came with me through eight startups. Here are his words:

> I was hired into Caremark as a communications person away from the prestigious advertising firm J. Walter Thompson. I had moved up quickly but left because I wanted my life to count for more than producing typical corporate advertising. There is nothing wrong with that, but selling cheese singles didn't light me up.
>
> I interviewed at Caremark, and someone other than Jim hired me. It turned out that there was a restructuring before I started, and I got assigned to Jim without him even meeting me. I probably looked fourteen at the time, but he welcomed me into his circle anyway. In my first week, he invited me to sit in on a media interview he was doing by phone.

The reporter asked, "What are the benefits of being cared for at home?"

Jim knew the answer backward and forward, so he responded, "Home is where patients do better. They're happier, and they get their lives back. It's a fraction of the cost of care. They're not exposed to the dangers of infections and other risks that aren't necessary unless they really need to be in the hospital. If they do, that's great. But if they no longer do, it is safer, cheaper, and more enjoyable to get care at home than in the hospital."

It was all true.

Then Jim added, "And actually, we take care of them better because hospital staff are busy, they can get distracted, and they don't really know as much about total parenteral nutrition as we do."

That may have also been true, but it made me cringe. Jim finished the call and turned to me. "Well, Larry, how did you like that?"

I took the risk of responding honestly, "I loved most of it."

Jim followed up with, "Tell me more. What didn't you love?"

I thought, *This may be the shortest tenure a communications person has ever had.*

> But I took a deep breath and said, "Jim, about a quarter of our referrals come from hospitals. Even if it's true that we can take care of these patients better than the hospitals, we don't need to be critical of the care they provide. That will not win us any friends, and it's not necessary."[1]
>
> He just looked up, nodded, and said, "Understood."
>
> That was the end of it. And Jim never did anything like that again. My suggestion didn't faze him in the slightest. If he hears something that is immediately persuasive, that's how it is going to be.

TELL ME MORE

Larry's story exemplifies how the phrase "tell me more" has worked well for me. It's not defensive. Another powerful question is, "What am I missing?"

These questions lead to answers, and answers provide vision. These phrases are easy to learn and powerful to use. If you make them a habit, you'll be miles ahead of most people. Train yourself by practicing.

If you want to stay alive in business, your ears had better be way bigger than your mouth. Your most important job is to listen.

If someone tells you about a problem they are having, you should not respond with, "Here's what you ought to do."

---

1 Larry Watts. Personal interview with the authors. November 10, 2022.

Instead, invite them to process it by saying, "Tell me more." Good coaches use the Socratic method, allowing mentees to arrive at answers by themselves.

When you say, "Tell me more," you will be amazed by how much comes pouring out of people. When you rigorously ask, "What am I missing?" you gain the insights you need. This kind of openness takes humility.

STARTING WITH A HYPOTHESIS

Whenever I have an idea, I start with a hypothesis, not a certainty. I like to express curiosity in the form of, "I wonder if. . . ."

Begin with a hypothesis and then seek data that will either validate your idea or not. I have never started a company because I thought something was a good idea. I've only launched after getting enough objective validation that the fundamentals were solid. Embrace the scientist's ethic of taking in data while remaining non-judgmental. A scientist considers opposing perspectives—the peer-review process confirms it.

The scientific method of testing ideas and making discoveries may be one of the most valuable skills of our day, given how rapidly human knowledge is progressing. In *Think Again*, Adam Grant eloquently states, "Intelligence is traditionally viewed as the ability to think and learn. Yet, in a turbulent world, there's another set of cognitive skills that might matter more: the ability to rethink and unlearn."[2] You can train yourself to do a remarkable thing: change your mind.

2 Grant, *Think Again*, 2.

I will give an example of when we started with a hypothesis before founding a company. It was called CardioNet, which pioneered the idea of continuous heart monitoring to diagnose issues. At the time, physicians would send patients home with a Holter Monitor to record their heart for twenty-four hours. After that period, the data would go out for analysis, which might take a month to get back. Patients sometimes died during that month. So, if something *had* occurred during the monitoring period, the report could tell a patient's family why they died—cold comfort after it's too late.

Most often, though, the data turned up nothing because more than a day is needed to catch intermittent problems. I hypothesized that new cell phone technologies could monitor someone's heart in real-time and would make doing so cost-effective. We started by asking physicians, "How much benefit might there be if we could do continuous monitoring for ten or thirty days compared to one day? What if you could see a million heartbeats instead of a hundred thousand?"

Here is what we learned:

- The average high-risk arrhythmia is detected on day nine. So, if you only monitor for one day, you only have a one-in-nine chance of catching it.
- 67 percent of arrhythmias are asymptomatic, which means you don't feel them.
- Heart conditions like this are life-threatening. The next time one happens, it could be a minor symptom, or it could be the big one that kills you. If you do survive, you might have severe damage.

> The cost of not preemptively treating these issues is extremely high.

We validated our premise that an extended monitoring period would save lives—a million heartbeats *is* better than a hundred thousand. At the time, however, Medicare would only reimburse for a day. We thought that needed to change. The more I looked into it, the more incensed I became with the status quo. Why should we wait a month only to have the patient die and then diagnose the cause after the fact? There is a better way. We could intercede at the very moment when a patient has a particular type of tachycardia and do something about it.

The answer to our initial question was head-slappingly obvious. "Yeah, of course it would be better to watch someone's heart for a longer period of time."

Okay, so the idea was right, but was it practical? Industry experts had doubts, pointing out logistical reasons why it couldn't be done. I listened attentively and chased down the concerns but found that none of their objections presented an insurmountable challenge. The central premise was validated, and we believed we could overcome the hurdles. It was time for more tests.

We worked out a business model where a monitoring center watched data from patients in real time, ranked by the most critical situations. If the algorithm detected a life-threatening event, one of our employees called the patient's physician, even in the middle of the night. You can imagine how the call might begin with an awakened doctor cursing the intrusion but ended with "Thank you. I'm so glad you called."

In the case of CardioNet, the hypothesis was validated, but what do you do when the outcome *doesn't* support the hypothesis? An inspiring example comes from British physicist Andrew Lyne. He published a major discovery and was scheduled to present his findings to peers at a conference. In the meantime, he realized he had overlooked a critical variable, and his calculations were wrong...horribly wrong. Instead of trying to skirt the issue, he walked onto the stage and admitted his mistake to hundreds of colleagues. Rather than attacking him, the room erupted into a spontaneous standing ovation. A fellow physicist called it, "the most honorable thing I have ever seen."[3]

During the experimentation phase, your beliefs must stay flexible. If a hypothesis is rejected, you move on to the next. As you pan the landscape, you may see that conditions are changing. In that event, jump on a chair quickly because the music is about to stop.

COACHING OTHERS

At any given time, I am mentoring half a dozen people regarding their startups or through the Stephen Ministries. The odds are always long against any proposed venture working, but if you're not asking the right questions, the odds are pretty high that it won't. I ask myself the same kinds of questions if I am considering a new idea. Then I bounce it off others.

3 Grant, *Think Again, 73.*

This process is like peeling back the layers of an onion. It usually takes repeating the phrase, "tell me more" several times before we get to the core of an issue. This approach is like the "five whys" problem-solving technique in manufacturing," originally developed by Sakichi Toyoda. This methodology asks iterative questions about why a malfunction or error occurred. Ultimately, a root cause emerges.[4]

Founders often have an attention-grabbing elevator pitch, but we must uncover whether an idea expands or bumps into a dead end. It's a process of triangulation to reach core issues.

Early in my career, I met Peter Lynch, the legendary manager of the Magellan fund at Fidelity Investments. He reviewed Caremark to determine whether he wanted to invest. He asked a handful of questions and quickly reached the nub of the issue. I was amazed to see his deftness in wielding questions, and he did end up investing. I understood that his seemingly intuitive process was grounded in a wealth of experience. In this way, the ability to ask great questions and then triangulate comes from pattern recognition.

It can also help when someone on the outside looks in and sees a blind spot that insiders have missed. An example comes to mind: I helped a talented marketing professional work on improving her business. Her clients loved her, but she worked about eighty hours a week. Her coping strategy was to take a seventy-two-hour respite about once a month, in which she would completely unplug to replenish her energy. She would

4 The "five whys" technique has been criticized as too simplistic for rigorous root-cause determination. However, the idea is easy to understand and is helpful in principle.

emerge ready to take up the fight again. She was getting by, but I worried she would burn out. Further, she desired more time for the nonprofit work that was important to her.

Looking at her situation from an objective perspective, I noticed she had not raised her billable rate in many years. She had minimal client turnover and was reluctant to charge her longtime clients more. I leveled with her that charging too little was robbing her time. If she raised her billable rate, she could hire someone to take on mundane tasks, providing better service and freeing her to do more of what she enjoyed most. She could orchestrate rather than play all the instruments by herself.

She implemented a rate increase of around 60 percent and didn't lose a single client. One even responded that they had begun feeling guilty about paying her too little. This marketing professional was not defensive when I brought this to her attention, and you shouldn't be either when someone shows you a blind spot.

I genuinely want to understand why someone might disagree with me. I'm obsessive about listening when people tell me I'm full of it. They usually have something meritorious to say and might possess an insight I need.

I have also learned not to get attached to my preferred outcome. When considering a venture, more often than not, we reach a place where we have to say, "This dog won't hunt." At those times, it's critical to pull the plug without delay. Beware, because emotions can keep you from doing what you already know you need to do. Prolonging a decision once you see a fatal flaw squanders precious time, energy, or resources. You might put off the inevitable because you don't want to hurt others, but drawing it out will usually hurt everyone more.

PREPARING FOR TOUGH QUESTIONS

Once you have sufficiently vetted your idea, you will shift from seeking counsel to an environment where you pitch your idea to others. For example, you might gain an audience with investors, customers, or employees. When you hear objections, you will tap into the deep listening you've already done.

My approach is to first listen to as many objections as possible from friendly sources such as a mentor or a prospect where the outcome is inconsequential. And I do mean as many as possible. I want to hear every question before I am on the spot.

Likewise, when I'm the mentor, I grill the startup team so they can field the toughest questions from me first. This exercise gives them a chance to rehearse in a friendly setting.

Another approach is first to pitch a customer, partner, or target where the stakes are low before setting your sights on the one you really want. For example, when I first sought investment for Caremark, I worked through every venture capital firm where I could get an appointment. I used each rehearsal opportunity before meeting with the one I wanted: Kleiner Perkins. They were the most prestigious Silicon Valley firm then, and I sought their expertise and credibility to help catapult Caremark forward. By that time, I had gone through so many practice runs, I knew what investors would ask, and I had answers ready.

At Kleiner Perkins, the partners grilled me for days, and I answered every one of their questions, a feat they later told me no other founder had been able to do. They finally gave me the nod. It worked out well for all of us and was a decision that Frank Caufield later said made him his first million (followed by hundreds of millions during his career). I followed this pattern in subsequent years to prepare for any press conference, investment round, or big client meeting.

In the appendix, I have included what I call The Contrarian's Checklist—a tool to work through testing your ideas. It contains the questions I would ask about your venture if you and I could sit down together. That checklist comes from years of doing this with founders.

FEAR PREVENTS LISTENING

Let's pause for a moment to do some self-analysis. Think about a time when someone provided you with feedback that was hard to hear. How did you reply? What were the sensations you felt in your body? Did you lash out or argue? Did you defend yourself? Did you shut down?

In other words, when challenged, is your typical reaction to fight or to flee? The book *Crucial Conversations: Tools for Talking When Stakes Are High* refers to these reactions as either "silence or violence."[5] Neither one is productive because they are based on fear of rejection, uncertainty, or failure. We dis-

5 Joseph Grenny, Kerry Patterson, Ron McMillan, Al Switzer, and Emily Gregory, *Crucial Conversations: Tools for Talking When Stakes Are High, (New York: McGraw Hill, 2002), 51.*

cussed in Chapter One that this is natural when the ego feels threatened.

So, how can you learn to calm yourself and take in the data offered?

Remember that an immediate reply is not needed or helpful when people give you feedback. Instead, adopt an open attitude of curiosity. Data is not an attack on you. You are gaining valuable intelligence. Consider it friendly assistance so you can see the potholes ahead.

Another tool is learning to pay attention to your body in these circumstances. Doing so will kick your thinking mind into action and help you make physiological corrections. Notice what is happening with you. Is your body language open or closed? Are your muscles relaxed or tense? Do your cheeks feel hot? Are you breathing? Remember that cognitive functions constrict when you're not getting enough oxygen to your brain. If you find yourself tensing up, physically open your posture. Lean forward. Smile. Breathe. Ask genuine questions to show your openness and shift your logical brain into gear. Train yourself to pause and sincerely say, "I am listening." If you use this phrase and mean it, you'll be amazed by the reactions from others. People are unaccustomed to being genuinely listened to, and it can have a disarming effect. Using this phrase will also ground you, so try it. Practice it often.

How can you stay calm when you receive unsettling facts? Consider that the best approach in the moment may be to postpone any reaction at all. Instead, sleep on it. Then, try processing it with a wise sounding board, someone invested in your success.

Another way to stay grounded is to ask questions. When you ask a question, you enter a more intellectually driven state. Then, the body's fight-or-flight symptoms cool, blood returns to the brain, and you can better examine the issue.[6]

DON'T DEVELOP THICK SKIN

You might hear that you should develop thick skin after receiving feedback, but this can be terrible advice. Armor is counterproductive if it prevents information from getting through to you. So, rather than blocking input or becoming impervious to it, train yourself to have a strong rebound.[7] Figure out strategies to regroup your emotional energy in a positive way. Consider that sensitivity and openness might be one of your superpowers, so it's okay to acknowledge that someone's words stung. The goal is to turn creative insecurity into your benefit, not build walls against it.

Next, consider whether the feedback was on point or ill-founded. Is there a kernel of truth you need to see? Please do not block the information from getting through to you. Refrain from biting back, because if you do, people will eventually stop communicating with you.

These habits are not always easy to master, but we can all train our bodies, minds, and language so we can respond with the positive reflexes outlined in this section.

---

6 Grenny, et al., *Crucial Conversations, 49.*

7 Tiffany Hawk, "Writers And Rejection: Why You Don't Need A Thicker Skin," https://www.tiffanyhawk.com/blog/why-you-dont-need-a-thicker-skin, accessed June 17, 2024

In summary, realize that hard data is only one type of input. I take it all in, even if some of it is ambiguous.

Recognize that making good decisions involves:

1. The data itself
2. Interpretation of the data
3. Reaction to the data

Start with data, then interpret it through a process of triangulation. This involves sensing what you think will happen, even if you can't put your finger on why you have that hunch. As I gather feedback, I certainly listen to what experts say, but I don't put undue weight on naysaying. Be aware of concerns and pitfalls, but your instincts should carry the day.

In this spirit, I like the counsel given by author Tiffany Hawk, who coaches writers with this advice she once heard. It is, "Don't be a feedback bitch."[8] By that, she means that immediately jumping to it when someone critiques your work isn't healthy. Consider their suggestions, but the decision is ultimately yours. Your voice is unique and valuable. Don't let an editor scrub out your personality. And don't assume other people know best or that they have your same interest at heart.

Finally, your reaction to the data involves taking the next step. After you have taken in data and discussed that input, there comes a moment when your decision becomes clear. At that moment, it's your job to say, "I've heard what you have said. We've looked at it from different angles. Now, here is what we will do, and this is why."

---

8 Tiffany Hawk, *Breakthrough Book Proposal online course, March 2023.*

This is when your entrepreneurial vision coalesces into leadership. Then, end the debate. Move forward. Do it in an unemotional way. There will be tradeoffs. Some people may not like it. The path may be difficult, but take the necessary steps with focused discipline.

Act decisively and insist on unity among your team. One hallmark of great companies is that team members may debate vigorously, but once a decision is made, everyone rallies to make the plan a success, even if they had once disagreed with it.[9]

A TELESCOPIC BRAIN

In addition to asking, "What am I missing?" and listening to their instincts, visionaries can pan out and see the big picture, then zoom in on details to make a plan of attack. This way of thinking comes with practice.

When grappling with a thorny problem, pause and come back to it later to see it with fresh eyes. Vision means seeing issues from multiple angles. Sculptors and artists have a technique of putting a mirror in front of their work so they can see it in reverse. The reflection helps them spot issues that their brains have been correcting. Likewise, learn to look from different perspectives. Get out of your office and do some good old MBWA—management by walking around.

My colleague, Bill Long, described vision this way: "Vision means, 'I think I can get from here to there. And "there" is

---

9 Jim Collins and Morten T. Hansen, *Great by Choice: Uncertainty, Chaos, and Luck—Why Some Thrive Despite Them All, (New York: Harper Collins, 2011), Kindle Edition, 167.*

pretty far away.' The whole picture is, 'I actually understand how hard this will be.' Vision doesn't mean you have all the answers."[10]

Bill added this about how we zoomed in on the details: "It was not that hard to figure out that you can deliver intravenous therapy outside the hospital. But then you start thinking about specifics. How many patients are there? How do we find them? What is their home environment? How do we control that? That type of vision comes from experience. It's not just seeing the big picture but also the interconnections of the big picture. It's not just moving forward with energy or vision. But moving forward with maturity."

I wasn't born with telescopic vision; I learned it by working in healthcare for twenty years before starting Caremark. Now that I've been through more than a dozen successful startups, I can apply that experience to help founders in other industries. Sound business principles apply across industries, while subject matter experts are best at analyzing specific use cases.

PREPARE YOUR SUMMATION FROM THE FIRST MEETING

I once worked with an attorney who did not lose cases, and he taught me something worth remembering. From the first meeting with his client, he began working on his closing arguments to the jury. He started with the summation and worked backward from there.

That is how I work too. Vision is a mindset of beginning each journey with where you want to go and then planning

10 Bill Long. Personal interview with authors, October 6, 2022

the route accordingly. It's creating an endpoint and working backward without knowing how you will get there.

That is another way of reinforcing Stephen Covey's adage to begin with the end in mind.[11] Otherwise, you may fall into the trap Lewis Carroll wrote about in Alice in Wonderland, "If you don't know where you are going, any road can take you there."[12]

HAVING A VISION FOR YOUR LIFE

What if you lived your whole life by starting with the summation? I believe that one day, we must all account before God for our choices. What will your closing arguments be? What changes should you make today so you don't have regrets at the end of your life?

Harvard Business School professor Clayton Christensen was a good friend of mine and one the best men I have ever known. We spent time together in Boston putting together a fund for one of his projects. He was extraordinarily intelligent but did not let his intelligence take him over. He had a tremendous and positive impact on the healthcare community and wrote the book *The Innovator's Dilemma*, which helps people understand the role of disruptive innovation across industries.

---

11 Steven Covey, *The 7 Habits of Highly Effective People, "Habit 2: Begin With the End in Mind* https://www.franklincovey.com/the-7-habits/habit-2/. Franklin Covey. Accessed June 7, 2024

12 Lewis Carroll, *Alice in Wonderland, Accessed from Goodreads* https://www.goodreads.com/quotes/642816-if-you-don-t-know-where-you-are-going-any-road, June 17, 2024

Cleveland Clinic CEO, Dr. Toby Cosgrove, said about that book, "When I picked it up, I just couldn't get enough of it. I decided I would go and see what I could learn from him. I was a great admirer." When I heard him say that, I thought about how like-minded people will attract.

Despite all Christensen's accomplishments, he never talked about them; instead, he was curious about what he could learn from other people. I saw him as a deeply religious family man who was the very embodiment of humility. His other book was *How Will You Measure Your Life*, which challenges each of us to imagine the end of our time on Earth and then work backward from the outcome we want. That is starting with the summation.

When he passed away in 2020, I doubt Clayton had many regrets. He had lived an exemplary life, the summation of which was an inspiration to me. I miss him.

CHAPTER 7

Landing on a Big Insight

In a twist of fate, in 1990, I found myself occupying the very office where I made the presentation to McGaw that led to me getting fired. I had assembled an investor group and learned that McGaw was on the auction block. McGaw was a minor player in IV solutions against the fierce competitors Baxter and Abbott Laboratories. McGaw only held 10 percent of the market share, and the others each held about 45 percent. Their positions hadn't changed in years because each company had signed long-term contracts with hospitals that locked the others out of their turf.

When McGaw went up for sale, I wanted it because I saw a way to make an end run around those hospital contracts with a new service. I knew hospital pharmacies were mixing IV solutions in-house and dispensing them to patients. Keep in mind that about 85 percent of IV drips are hung to deliver drugs. This process was a challenge for hospitals because their pharmacies are high-demand environments, and these solutions require careful measuring, ideally, under sterile conditions. My idea was to create a series of central admixture pharmacies that would compound these solutions on demand and deliver them to hospitals, thereby alleviating a burden. I knew we could build a controlled environment that would ensure the sterility of these drips.

The end run around the contracts was that we would not technically be selling the solutions themselves, we would be selling the service of mixing and delivering the solutions. This idea was my secret weapon in acquiring McGaw. So, I called the investment banker in charge of the sale, a man by the name of Alberto Cribiore. I said, "Don't sell to anybody else." He said, "You're too late. There are a dozen other suitors in line ahead of you." I then told him we would pay more, which we could afford to do because of the secret weapon up my sleeve. We were the thirteenth group that wanted to acquire McGaw, but we hammered out a deal.[1]

Afterward, our team needed to launch this service and convince hospitals to outsource this part of their business. Fortunately, although McGaw was a smaller player, it had a stellar reputation for high ethics and quality. Its sales team was well-liked in the industry. We had a lot going for us. Still, this was a new concept, and anything new is an uphill battle. We needed to get the hospital pharmacists to see us as a valuable resource and not competition—no small feat.

We went to work on how we would prime them for our launch. We decided to begin with a deep dive into what made

---

1 We increased the value of McGaw by 650 percent in three years after it had been relatively flat for the previous sixty years. I attribute the success of this acquisition partially to the fact that we gave all the employees stock, partly to hiring an entrepreneurial management team after letting the existing team go, and of course, to the "secret weapon" of starting our central admixture pharmacy services (CAPS).

pharmacists tick, so we did a series of interviews. I already sensed hospital pharmacists felt undervalued, and they repeatedly returned to that theme in the interviews. Here was a highly educated group of professionals relegated to the hospital basement. It was a relentless production environment where physicians and nurses demanded their orders immediately, or "stat!" in medical terms. In a word, what pharmacists wanted was respect. They wanted to be more involved with patient care because they had chosen a career in medicine to make a difference.

We had the idea to create a video for the annual meeting of the American Society of Hospital Pharmacists in Las Vegas in January, but we only had a couple of months to do it. We didn't want to make a dull, self-centered corporate video. Our marketing team made fun of those, calling them (in a snooty voice) "the pride and the promise." We wanted our video to be a gift from us that would elevate the status of pharmacists and pharmacy techs.

So, we hired a team to make a music video set to the tune of Aretha Franklin's "Respect." For the lyrics, we gleaned direct quotes we'd heard from pharmacists and their technicians about the relentless demands they faced and the degrading treatment they endured. Those catchy lyrics came from a place of deep listening.

Nowhere in the video did we talk about what we were about to launch. It was 100 percent about the pharmacists. It said, without saying it: "We get you." "We respect you." We approached pharmacists from the "you-point-of-view," a concept we will address in Chapter 11. We heard them when they said, "I'm frustrated. Nobody understands what I'm doing. Politics get in the way of my ability to serve patients."

After all the listening we had done, we'd gained and validated a simple insight: respect. This knowledge hailed to The Marketing Concept, which can be distilled down to this: Ask people what they want and give it to them.

With validation in hand, it was time to invest, so we poured a small fortune into the video production. By the time we watched the final cut, we knew it would be a home run. It wasn't a gamble; it was a calculated investment. We got ready for the annual meeting, where we would air it. We got Jay Leno to keynote our event. He was one of the most famous personalities of the day as host of the *Tonight Show*, and he would draw our audience into the room.

Leno was brilliant. He opened with some funny lines and then played the video. It brought the house down—the crowd went wild.

Then he did something genius. He read the room's energy, set aside what he had prepared—set aside his ego—and asked, "Do you want to see it again?"

The crowd roared, "Yes!"

Leno made the moment about them. He gave them what they wanted. And he also served us, who had hired him. We were grateful.

That video unleashed a pent-up passion in those pharmacists, and they began requesting copies and showing the clip to everyone they knew. That video became a standard part of pharmacy school curriculum across the country and would remain so for decades. You can still find it on YouTube.

When we finally launched our "Central Admixture Pharmacy Services," or CAPS for short, the pharmacists listened to us because we had listened to them first.

THE BIG INSIGHT

This story shows how we landed on a big insight through intensive listening. Insights like that are central to vision. There comes a moment of clarity when you have a breakthrough. This insight is so compelling that people immediately understand it. Your revelation might come from data, but more often, it will emerge organically from a deep understanding of your customers. Intensive listening is the fastest way to get there. Early in a project, I'd rather do a handful of in-depth interviews with my prospective customers than get five hundred surveys.

While we paid a premium to buy McGaw, we sold it for six and a half times our purchase price three and a half years later. All this came from reshaping the jungle by going around the hospital IV contracts with premixed solutions.

Vision involves asking, "Why can't I do this? What do I have to test to validate whether I'm right or not?" Then, you iterate that process until you get to the heart of what matters. Once you have that, you can be confident you are right. You are ready to bet on it.

WHAT MAKES A GOOD VISION?

How do you know if the vision you have is one worth pursuing? A good vision is big enough to be worth your time. It's simple and easy to explain. It comes from a quiet understanding of where you have the potential to be world class. What you can be the best at doesn't come from a place of bravado but a calm realization of your strengths and market potential.

A good vision also springs from a place of love and the desire to serve others. I've never met anyone who became successful because they wanted to get rich. Conversely, I've met plenty of people who are successful because they want to improve the outcome of something. They want to make the world better. In doing so, they might make a lot of money, but that is not the objective. What I have always cared about is impact. When you are driven by service, your work will be self-rewarding.

Check your motive. *Why are you doing this?*

Here are three more guidelines for a good vision:

- Don't major in the minors.
- Keep it simple, genius.
- Develop a simple story.

DON'T MAJOR IN THE MINORS

The place to start is by asking yourself, is this a big idea or a small idea? A big idea and a small idea take the same amount of time, so pick a big one. Devote your energy to solving problems that people have an intense need to fix, that will dramatically improve their lives, and where a vast market exists.

I am looking for billion-dollar ideas. As I said above, money is not the most meaningful metric, but I do want to see an impact on that scale. I will repeat that it isn't about getting rich; it's about solving a problem with that type of impact. When you are solving a momentous problem, customer gratitude will fuel your fire. It will be fun, and others will want to join. All these outcomes will make the work self-motivating.

Most people think that small, incremental gains will be easier, but I have observed that people tend to stick with changes that make a real difference. Meaningful changes will reset your life and become self-motivating. You never want to go back to the way you were before.

The principle of majoring in the majors is another way of explaining Pareto's Law, or the 80-20 rule, which states that 80 percent of the benefits will come from 20 percent of projects or customers. It is a rule of thumb, and in the book *The ONE Thing*, Gary Keller takes the idea further. He says to whittle your focus down from 20 percent to one big thing at any time or in any part of your life. The human mind can only effectively concentrate on one hard thing at once, and there is tremendous waste in shifting from one task to another. Keller asks this clarifying question, "What's the one thing I can do, such that by doing it, everything else will be easier or unnecessary?"[2]

I agree. Once you have validated that one thing, double down on it. Stop worrying about the noise. Keller says you must come to terms with a certain amount of chaos outside that one thing. Notifications and minor tasks will pile up

2 Gary Keller and Jay Papasan, *The ONE Thing: The Surprisingly Simple Truth About Extraordinary Results, Rellek Publishing Partners, Ltd, 2013), Audible Audiobook edition, 5 hr. 28 min.*

while you are majoring in the majors. Many tasks don't ever need to get done. In coaching, I remind people to get out of the weeds and focus on what is essential. I might ask, "Tell me why you picked that as something you want to work on. How important is that to the overall strategy?"

My longtime colleague Larry Watts described it this way, "Pick something that is just screaming out to God for change. Not a mild improvement, not a 'well, it could be a little bit better.' You're looking for a problem that currently costs five times as much and where people have a terrible quality of life."[3]

Make sure you are addressing the kind of need Larry described. Too many startups are solutions looking for a problem.

In evaluating an idea, I also ask how big the total market size is if you were to capture 100 percent of it. Your focus is too narrow if the top number is too small. Next, look for a niche without meaningful competition where you can be a monopoly of one.

Then, examine ways that your idea can have natural offshoots. I ask, "Is this a product or a business?" One mistake is that entrepreneurs launch a business around a single good idea. It is a good product, but the outgrowth potential is limited.

The advice I give founders when I see them getting too far into minutiae is reminding them to stay maniacally focused on the big insight, the big goal. Filter out what is extraneous. In my projects, I spend considerable time trying to get to the

3 Watts, Larry. Personal interview with the authors. September 1, 2022.

core issue versus what is interesting but not critical. It takes real effort to differentiate between the two.

We met all the above criteria for a big idea when we created the high-tech home healthcare industry. Our product prevented death. Our efforts saved billions of dollars and gave patients their lives back. The market was practically unlimited and growing because of an aging population and because we could grow high-tech home healthcare as an overall segment.

For all the reasons outlined in this section, I believe it is even *easier* to solve a big problem than a small problem.

ONE MEANINGFUL EXAMPLE: THE HUMAN VALUE OF A BIG IDEA

In my founder role, I wasn't on the front lines of delivering patient care, so I never got to meet many people helped by our products. But a few months ago, one came along in a way that moved me.

When I relocated to El Paso, I became involved with the Church of St. Clement, and they have a Stephen Ministry there. I had gone through the training in Austin, so I picked a church where I could continue with this service.

They have four Stephen Ministry leaders, two of whom I met and two of whom I had not. One of the leaders, named Diana Orrantia, was a retired math professor. Diana was part of a vetting process, and I met her for an interview.

She formally began by saying, "Tell me about yourself." I shared some of my professional experience. After a moment, she stopped me and said, "Mr. Sweeney...." I then stopped her and said, "No, please, call me Jim."

She continued, "Jim, I've done a deep dive on you, and you've saved my life two times."

I was stunned and said, "Really? Tell me more."

Her story brought me to tears.

Years before, I'd worked with MD Anderson to create a home program for them. It turns out Diana had been a cancer patient there. She told me this:

> One of the main reasons I was able to manage my leukemia was because of Caremark. The treatment allowed me to become ambulatory, get out of the hospital, and stay in an apartment. Before that, I had been in the hospital for a month. Soon after I arrived at MD Anderson, they released me to live in Houston for the next year. They put an extended PICC line in my arm so I could walk around.
>
> You enabled me to receive home care and live a somewhat normal life outside the hospital. I just wanted to thank you because you were a huge reason why I was able to smile, and why I was able to spend time with my family. The companies you began made it possible for me to not be in the hospital that whole time, which was wonderful for my quality of life.

She went on to say that after receiving a bone marrow transplant, she started having heart palpitations. They placed her on a CardioNet monitor, which found the problem.

Because she got round-the-clock monitoring of her heart, she could remain home. This was the second life-saving technology she referred to when we met.

Everyone will define success in their own way; it's something that you experience internally. But to me, success is identifying your personal brass ring and taking on its risks and failures. Success is continuing to fail until you get your brass ring. Hearing Diana's story shows what success feels like to me. It felt appropriate to share that story in this chapter to illustrate what it looks like to major in the majors. Do something with your life that is so meaningful that customers can bring tears to your eyes. That's why this book is dedicated to her.

Once you have launched your company, stay focused on the big picture. Choose tasks and projects that yield the most benefit. Remember to check out The Contrarian's Checklist in the appendix for more guidance to help vet your big ideas.

KEEP IT SIMPLE, GENIUS

People use the acronym KISS for "keep it simple, stupid," which is catchy and memorable. However, I take issue with the language because simplicity isn't stupid, it's genius. Anyone can make something complex but paring it down to its elegant essence is brilliant.

I'll tell you about a product idea that I think is simple and genius: dental flossers. These solve a problem that everyone has. We all know we need to floss, but the old type of floss is a pain to use and cuts into your fingers. Whoever invented the new flosser picks deserves a medal.

Another classic example was how the iPod solved a problem people didn't know they had. Its claim to fame was its ability to store 1,000 songs in your pocket. That was a concept people could immediately grasp and one that they wanted.

When we hired Jay Leno to come and emcee our debut of the video, we were building a whole product launch around a single word: respect. That word became a guiding philosophy that remains with me today. It's an elegantly simple idea and a vitally important one.

Less is more. Dialing in your message is a fun challenge. Stay on it until your delivery sings. Here is a quote by Antoine de Saint-Exupéry from *Wind, Sand and Stars* that sums up the idea: "Perfection is finally obtained not when there is no longer anything to add, but when there's no longer anything to take away."[4]

DEVELOP A STORY

When you explain your idea, break it into simple components. That's how you raise money. Tell stories to illustrate those components in a straightforward, relatable form. Compelling stories keep your message relevant. Stories take people's guard down as they listen and relate.

I remember first realizing I needed to become a better storyteller after having the experience early in my career of someone looking at me and saying, "Sweeney, I have no idea what you're talking about." I pondered where I had gone wrong. I

4 Quoted by Rick Rubin, *The Creative Act: A Way of Being, (New York: Penguin, 2023), 243-244.*

concluded that I needed to tell stories to help people see what I was trying to communicate. People forget facts, but they remember stories.

Pick a real person to illustrate your story. Early in Caremark, we found a world-class photographer named Deborah Myers. We convinced her to take on the job of going around the country to photograph people using our home IV solutions. She was a luminous person who connected well with others and developed a relationship with people when she took their portrait.

One of the people she interviewed was a woman by the name of Lily Mae Pledger. Deborah got to know Lily Mae as she was setting up the shot and learned that she lived in poverty and only had an elementary school education. But Lily Mae learned how to mix her own IV solutions and administer them perfectly. She learned how to compound twenty-six ingredients into an IV using sterile techniques and place it into her superior vena cava, which is a major vessel leading to the heart. It was such a concentrated solution that it had to go directly to the heart. If it got contaminated, it would most likely have killed her. It was dangerous, but she did it.

I can still see in my mind's eye how doctors would look at me with their arms folded, saying, "Jim, you have a great idea, but *these people* won't be able to figure out how to do this."

When they said, "these people," I could hear the tone that meant, "these idiot patients." It was the same condescending attitude that the pharmacists felt from doctors.

The antidote was respect. I believed Lily Mae was capable. That was a contrarian opinion. My thesis, which turned out to be accurate, was to put myself in the patient's shoes: I'm a patient. I don't want to be shackled to a hospital for the rest of my life. So, I have a huge motivation to do this on my own and to not do it wrong.

Whose motivation is greater, the patient's or the hospital's staff? I could imagine workers chatting about their weekend plans while mixing solutions. This wasn't a stretch—I had seen as much.

Lily Mae Pledger became our best poster child. We published her picture and others in our first annual report, which helped convince new hospitals to take a chance on change. Those large-format portraits projected a sense of dignity. Those photographs humanized the patients, and they hang in my office to this day. Keats said, "Truth is Beauty. Beauty Truth." Those portraits are beautiful in every sense.

We had data and facts to share, but seeing Lily Mae was more compelling than any of that. That's what I mean by developing a story to share your vision with others. Keep it simple and put a human face to it.

As a postscript to that story, the photographer, Deborah Myers, came from a family of doctors, but she had rebelled as a young woman and became a world-renowned photographer instead. Then something unexpected happened. As she interviewed our patients and took their photographs, it kindled something inside her, and she decided to suspend her full-time photography business to become a physician. Today, she is a marvelous doctor and runs a cardiology unit at the University Hospital System in Portland, Oregon. Patients say she is the best doctor they have ever had.

CHAPTER 8

THE NO-QUIT GENE

In 1953, a fledgling startup called Rocket Chemical Company in my hometown of San Diego set out to create a rust-prevention solvent. They tried and failed. Tried again and failed. It took forty failures before they got the formula right, which they named Water Displacement 40, or WD-40. Today, that useful product is in 176 countries, and most American households have multiple cans. They do over a hundred million dollars in annual revenue as of the writing of this book. If they had given up on the thirty-ninth try, we wouldn't have WD-40 today.[1]

Thomas Edison's famous quote comes to mind here too. When pressed to report results or explain his progress, he said: "I have not failed. I've just found 10,000 ways that won't work."[2]

That's what I call failing your way to success. One less step is failure. One more is success. This type of indefatigability is the no-quit gene. This "gene" is present in everyone; the ques-

1 WD-40, *Fascinating Facts You Never Learned in School, (*https://www.wd40.com/history/), accessed June 24, 2024

2 Thomas Edison, "Famous Quotes by Thomas Edison," Foundationhttps://www.thomasedison.org/edison-quotes, accessed June 20, 2024

tion is whether it is active or latent in you. This trait can be trained and strengthened. This chapter explores what this type of indefatigability looks like and how to develop it.

You remember the cliche, "If at first you don't succeed, try, try again." My kids remember me telling them a modified version. "If at first you don't succeed, try a thousand times."

NEAR-DEATH EXPERIENCES IN COMPANIES

I have yet to start a company that didn't have two or three near-death experiences before it was successful. That's part of being a startup, but it can be demoralizing for folks in the middle of a near-death experience. They can't believe they tried something, and it didn't work.

I don't care why or how we made a mistake; I don't care why we are where we are. That's history, and I can't change it. I want to know what to do about it. It's astounding how many people hold on to why they are where they are, trying to deflect blame. It was a hard habit for people to overcome when they came into our organization from elsewhere.

I'll give an example. A bid process had opened with the Veteran's Administration to supply our product, and we successfully won that contract away from a competitor. This contract then became half of our overall business. In the meantime, our competitor wasn't happy about losing the contract, and they challenged the VA for awarding it to us. The crux of their challenge lay in pricing their product below cost, forcing the VA's hand; they had to reconsider. It was an unprecedented move, and they did it to bury our business. The VA took the bait, and in an instant, we lost the contract.

I went to our regulatory affairs person with the news, and he said, "Don't worry about it. Let's wait, and we'll take the issue to Washington."

I said, "We are absolutely not going to wait. We will deal with this here and now." I went straight to the VA and made our case that we had a superior product with bags made from a biologically inert material that did not leach chemicals into the patient's body or into the environment. Our competitor's bags used plasticizers, but our clean bags aligned with the VA's goal of promoting environmentally responsible practices.

We also restructured our bid and were successful in winning the business back, which was unheard of. We were proactive, not waiting for the regulatory affairs people to sort it out in Washington. This account was the lifeblood of our business. The no-quit gene in me kicked in, and we turned it around.

FAILURES ARE JUST A SPEED BUMP

Failures aren't failures; they just slow you down temporarily. A setback doesn't keep you from reaching your destination. Often, people think you're either a failure or you're a success. I'm convinced that failure is embedded in success. The two are inextricably intertwined. I don't care how often I fail because I know I'm failing on my way to success. When I discover I'm wrong, I change. I don't get defensive or emotional about it. Nelson Mandela, the late revolutionary leader said, "I never lose. I either win or I learn."[3]

---

3 Jim Schleckser, "Nelson Mandela's Secret to Winning," *Inc. Magazine, June 21, 2016,* https://www.inc.com/jim-schleckser/nelson-mandela-s-secret-to-winning.html.

When you see a musician or athlete deliver what looks like an effortless performance, you don't see the thousands of hours of hard practice where they stretched well beyond their skill level. You don't know how many times they got injured or how flawed their early tries were.

Alex Honnold, the free-solo climber we mentioned earlier, describes failing your way to success this way: "The majority of the time you spend sport climbing, you're failing: falling off and then trying to figure out how not to fall. Climbing reminds you that to get better at anything, you've got to put in a tremendous amount of time and effort to keep beating your head against a wall to figure it out."[4]

When you admire a great company, you don't see all times they almost didn't make it. What matters is that they kept after it and continually pushed themselves to higher performance after reaching each new plateau.

A Japanese proverb says, "Fall seven, rise eight."[5]

As I've already said, the most significant opportunity of my life came the day I got fired. Failure is positive because it can cause you to reevaluate your assumptions. It prevents you from losing objectivity. Defeat gives you the chance to see something you missed before.

Embracing failure is the key to success. I fail every day. It's a beautiful thing, but I see too many people paralyzed by their fear of failure. They know what they need to do, but they are afraid. They think failure should be avoided at all costs, but

---

4 Harrell, "Life's Work, Alex Honnold."

5 Angela Duckworth, *Grit: The Power of Passion and Perseverance*, (New York: Scribner, 2016), Kindle Edition, 169.

we can all learn to recognize it as a healthy part of the process. We can look for the learning in each stumble. Some venture capital firms are known for only funding founders who have failed in the past.

NEVER RING THE BELL

I grew up in San Diego where Navy SEALs train, and I've long been fascinated by the program, which embodies the no-quit gene. SEAL trainees are the best of the best, and most will not make it. Throughout the program, trainees can quit by ringing a bell at any time, which would end their suffering. Between 70 and 80 percent don't make it, and this is after the program admits only about 1 percent of the soldiers in the Navy. The idea is to find those who would rather die than ring that bell. Those men would never give up on their team or the mission.

In your life and business, there are many endeavors you should quit, which we will discuss further in Chapter 10. But never ring the bell on yourself. Never give up on your values or your biggest dreams.

Singer Tina Turner left an abusive relationship and was not in demand as a solo artist. She fought through an ugly divorce and endured years of a lackluster solo career. She was cleaning toilets in Las Vegas and doing gigs at night to make ends meet. In an interview for the Harvard Business Review, she was asked, "You weren't immediately successful as a solo artist. Did you ever consider quitting?" This was her answer:

> I never considered giving up on my dreams. You could say I had an invincible optimism. And I always knew that the 'what' was more important than the 'how.' In other words, although I had a hard time seeing how I could make my dreams come true, I focused more on what I wanted to achieve in my life, personally and professionally. I took actions day-by-day, often outside my comfort zone, to better myself and bring me closer to those goals.[6]

She staged a comeback in her forties to become one of the top three recording artists of her day, along with Michael Jackson and Madonna. She had a guiding star, and it activated her no-quit gene.

One example of being indefatigable was that eight of the fourteen companies I started did not have approval for insurance reimbursement when we began. I first learned this the hard way with Caremark. My thinking early on was that our product made so much sense—being less expensive and better for the patient—so why *wouldn't* they reimburse for it? We got our first patient from the Cleveland Clinic, and I went to their insurance provider, which happened to be Blue Cross Blue Shield of Ohio. They promptly said, "We're not going to pay you."

---

6 Allison Beard, "Life's Work: An Interview with Tina Turner," *Harvard Business Review, January–February 2021,* https://hbr.org/2021/01/lifes-work-an-interview-with-tina-turner.

I didn't accept that answer. Instead, I learned that this employee worked at Ford Motor Company. So, I called Ford Motor Company and said, look, Blue Cross is not going to pay for this patient. It's going to be 'x' dollars if they stay in the hospital and 'y' dollars if you elect to use this treatment. They agreed with me, so someone at Ford called Blue Cross Blue Shield of Ohio. A few minutes later, we had an agreement to get paid. We then used that example to get other systems and insurers to reimburse us. Breaking that barrier each time was a laborious process, but we worked through it.

With those subsequent insurance companies, I learned there is a high risk you won't be reimbursed. If you aren't, you're sunk. I argued that they'd only have to pay half of what they were before, which was a win for them. Later, however, I was told by an insurance guy that one reason companies are reluctant to pay claims is because they're concerned about "The woodwork effect."

"What's that?" I asked.

He said, "If we pay for this, people will come out of the woodwork to get it, so we'll be paying out a lot more."

In other words, if a treatment is effective, more people will want it, and the insurer's costs will go up. They don't have such a big problem with ineffective treatments. It's one of the backwards incentives of healthcare funding.

We eventually got reimbursement approval for every one of my companies. But it wasn't easy, and that approval didn't always last. At Caremark, we achieved reimbursement, but later, Medicare decided they wouldn't reimburse us for part of our business. We had to write that off, and our stock value dropped by 90 percent in one day. That experience helped me realize that I am neither a hero nor a bum. I'm not the golden boy if our stock is on top, and I'm not the bum at the bottom of it. Sure, I had a bad day. But I didn't have a bad week or a bad month. I had a bad day, which led to me saying, "Okay, this happened. Now put your head down and work your way out of it."

That's what we did: we put eight successful consecutive quarters together. So, while the stock price had gone from thirty dollars a share to three, we brought it back from three dollars a share to forty-five. Those who stuck with the company—especially those who took a risk buying when the price was low—did very well. We later won that Medicare reimbursement back but at a reduced price.

The words of Winston Churchill in his famous commencement address are instructive: "This is the lesson: never give in, never give in, never, never, never, never—in nothing, great or small, large or petty—never give in except to convictions of honour and good sense. Never yield to force; never yield to the apparently overwhelming might of the enemy."[7]

PARENTING AND THE NO-QUIT GENE

If you are a parent, this is another area of your life where you may relate to the idea of failing your way to success. On any given day, it's easy to feel like a failure. But do we give up? No,

7 Winston Churchill, "Never give in, never, never, never." Speech, Harrow School, October 29, 1941, Accessed from https://www.nationalchurchill-museum.org/never-give-in-never-never-never.html, June 17, 2024

we keep trying imperfectly. All the traits of the contrarian's trifecta relate to parenthood. We have a vision of what our children are capable of and who they can become. We lean into humble insecurity and learn to listen intently. We appreciate how much our children teach us. We recognize when we are wrong and resolve to do better. On our best days, we coach with questions rather than lecturing with answers. We never give up on our desire to help them, and we catch ourselves when we see signs of fear-based toxic insecurity affecting our own behaviors. We make course corrections. We also never give up on their ability to grow. We keep trying, no matter how many times we may fail. Fall seven. Rise eight.

WHERE DO WE GET THE NO-QUIT GENE?

Are some people born indefatigable, or is this learned? Like most human traits, the answer is "yes and yes." I call it "the no-quit gene" because it's catchy, not because there is an actual gene. Everyone has the seeds of indefatigability, so the issue is whether it is latent or trained.

With human abilities, a person may be born with an innate talent, which is to say they learn specific skills more quickly than others. Talent and other genetic factors do matter, especially when it comes to elite levels of competition. Olympians need the body type for their sport to compete against others with the ideal body type for the sport. Possessing a knack for certain skills can make learning more enjoyable, which creates a positive feedback loop.

Work ethic is also partly learned. In both human and animal studies, creatures will default to laziness[8] because loafing serves the evolutionary purpose of saving energy. Research has shown that those who practice demanding tasks can overcome nature and translate work ethic gained from one endeavor into others. In other words, you can learn hard work.

In her book *Grit*, Angela Duckworth provides a roadmap for "learned industriousness," or, simply put, work ethic. Put yourself into environments where you work hard, are engaged, and have the chance to receive coaching. You will train muscles of perseverance, and your skills will improve. This also trains work ethic. [9]

I can't think of a better example of someone who failed his way to success than Dr. Toby Cosgrove, whom we mentioned in Chapter 3. While growing up, he struggled in school. He went to Williams College, and they had a language requirement. He thought, "I'd better take French because smart people speak French." He completed four semesters of remedial French five times a week. He came away with three D-minuses and a D. Because of poor grades, he was rejected by twelve medical schools before getting admitted.

Cosgrove completed medical school but ranked dead last among those who graduated with him. Because of his academic showing, he found himself unemployed for six months.

Then, he was sent to Vietnam, where he earned his stripes as a surgeon and soldier. He received a Bronze Star for his

---

8 Duckworth, *Grit, 240.*
9 Duckworth, *Grit, 240.*

medical work and a medal from the Vietnam government for a weekly clinic he ran on the side. He also flew combat missions "to keep busy."[10]

When he returned to the States, he began applying to residency programs but was repeatedly rejected again. He applied to Massachusetts General and decided to show up in person to get an appointment with the Chief of Surgery. Upon arrival, the secretary told him the Chief of Surgery was busy, so Cosgrove replied, "How about I sit here until he's got fifteen minutes?"[11]

That encounter landed him a job offer, which Cosgrove attributes to "just plain persistence and good luck."

At age thirty-four, Cosgrove learned about dyslexia, which explained his struggles in school. He has come to regard dyslexia as a gift. He said, "We're not very good at scholastic stuff, but we see other things that are different, and that's a big advantage." I agree. He has a far more innovative bend than many in similar positions.

Research says keen intelligence is often a hallmark of dyslexia. Neuroscientist Dr. Sally Shaywitz says, "There's a great deal to suggest that people who are dyslexic are not going to be your rote learners or bean counters." She adds, "They are going to be people to think outside of the box, to have vision, to move things forward."[12]

---

10 Solov, "From C's and D's to Clinic's helm."

11 Cosgrove, interview.

12 Sally Shaywitz, "Dyslexia: A new model of this reading disorder emphasizes defects in the language-processing rather than the visual system. It explains why some very smart people have trouble learning to read." (*Scientific American, November 1996, accessed from https://pages.ucsd.edu/~scoulson/CNL/shaywitz-dyslexia.pdf*

Once Cosgrove landed in a clinical setting, he thrived. He went on to become a world-renowned cardiologist, working with over twenty-two thousand patients in his career. He also became an accomplished inventor with eighteen patents.

At the age of sixty-four when most people start thinking of taking it easy, he was unanimously selected as the CEO of Cleveland Clinic. During his time there, Cleveland Clinic ranked as the number-two hospital system in the world behind Mayo Clinic. President Obama praised Cleveland Clinic and Mayo Clinic as providing "the highest quality care at well below the national norm" in terms of cost.

Under his leadership, Cleveland Clinic became the first medical school in the nation to be completely tuition-free. They now attract two thousand applicants for thirty-two positions, with quality on par with those who apply at Harvard Medical School. He implemented world-class quality initiatives, a radical transparency model, and created awards for innovation.

THE "FRAGILE PERFECTS"

We know that in cognitively demanding fields, there are no naturals. Not only does it take about ten thousand hours to become world-class, but it also takes ten thousand hours of *hard* practice.[13] Hard practice is not just exercising or dabbling but constantly pushing yourself beyond your natural limits. Expect it to be something other than sheer fun. Even

13 Malcom Gladwell *Outliers, (Hachette Audio, Audible audiobook version, 2008) 7 hr., 18 min.*

those passionate about the activity do not generally describe training as enjoyable. Their passion motivates them to endure hard training, and they can find it satisfying, but it does not eliminate suffering.[14]

Starting a business feels like hard practice. You love what you do and wouldn't stop doing it for anything, which gets you through the grueling hours and uncomfortable times.

The nature of hard practice involves working outside your current ability. Pushing beyond your limits is another form of leaning into insecurity. Can you embrace the pain to become stronger? Can you muscle through what it takes to grow your business through the near-death experiences, setbacks, and times when you make mistakes and get told no (again and again)? Can your ego take it when your stock price plummets?

One way to ensure you have the will to keep going is to experience failure and keep rising. Yes, that sounds like circular logic, but when you witness yourself getting up again after a dust-up, you see what you can finish. That knowledge is priceless and will change you forever.

Angela Duckworth calls the naturally talented people who have never been tested in the fire of adversity the "fragile perfects."[15] These people get into the best schools on account of their brilliance. The problem is that success came easily to them in the past, and they crumble when they face challenges too far outside their current abilities. These people ring the bell.

---

14 Duckworth, *Grit, Chapter 7, "Practice"*

15 Duckworth, *Grit, 190.*

As important as work ethic is, you must tap into something greater than willpower. To succeed long-term, you will need a deeper well of energy. What is that well?

My own experience tells me that it comes from two places. The first is that I love what I do. Call it passion. After I started my first company, I woke up and realized it no longer felt like work. When you no longer have to work to make a living, you're working because you choose to work. Then, it becomes a hobby. I haven't worked a day since I was thirty-six. I know it's cliché to say that, but it was a literal moment of realization for me.

Years ago, a colleague nicknamed me "The Energizer bunny" because I have never slowed down. I'm still energized long after the age that many people aim to retire. Why would I retire when I am doing what I love? I'm not working; I'm having a ball.

I am not the only entrepreneur to find satisfaction in the process. One consistent finding throughout the research on entrepreneurship is that people who work for themselves are far happier than others. One study says that the average person would have to earn two and a half times as much to be as happy working for someone else.[16]

Think of it in terms of someone who loves to go fishing. Nobody asks, "How long does it take to go fishing?" It's an absurd question because the point is not to get through it quickly and come home with a prize, but to enjoy the day. That's how I feel about building companies.

---

16 Malcolm Gladwell, "The Sure Thing," *The New Yorker, January 10, 2010, https://www.newyorker.com/magazine/2010/01/18/the-sure-thing.*

The second fuel source for my daily energy has been a sense of purpose. We discussed the notion of calling in Chapter 5. Once you find that calling, it adds a strength of will that you may not have known you had.

Don't start a business without a deep sense of purpose for something greater than yourself. You won't make it.

Current research mirrors my experience. Angela Duckworth's work on "grit" led her to interview people with exceptional stick-to-itiveness, whom she calls "paragons of grit." In doing so, she repeatedly heard, "I love what I do." Duckworth says, "nobody works doggedly on something they don't find intrinsically interesting.[17]

Duckworth also writes that purpose is a sense that "what I do matters to others." Passion is doing what you do for more than just yourself. She goes on to explain that anyone can have what might be described as "a job" or "a career" or "a calling." The latter is where you feel a degree of purpose.

These attitudes are not fixed; they often evolve with time, even in the same line of work. Your feelings about your employment can begin with interest in a topic and grow into passion.

Take heart if you want to find your passion but have yet to learn what that is. You can explore different interests. Many people don't realize their work will turn into passion when they first start, but they grow to love it for reasons they did not initially predict. Duckworth's research is especially instructive for young people who want to discover their interests and evolve from having a job to finding a calling in life.

---

17 Duckworth, *Grit, 106*

If you have entrepreneurial leanings but don't yet feel a deep sense of purpose, you might moonlight or dabble. Many people go from having a mere job to a career to a calling in this way. You may also join another entrepreneurial team to learn essential skills and gain experience. This environment may be foundational to preparing you to start your own business, or you may find yourself already in the right place to contribute. You might fall in love with that organization and achieve more as part of a team than you would as a founder. I don't believe everyone can or should start their own business. Please don't do it because you think you should. Only do it when you feel you must.

THE POWER OF POSITIVE THINKING

Positive thinking also plays a vital role in activating your no-quit gene. From the time I was a teenager, I have maintained a lifelong practice of repeating aphorisms and positively visualizing an outcome. Cynical people may reject these ideas as trite, but there is empirical evidence that it works. Angela Duckworth cites studies done on animals and meta-analysis of studies about human behavior. This research shows that people who believe they have control over their development try harder and are more persistent than those who see their traits as genetic.[18]

Her findings make sense. If you believe you may eventually find a solution, you'll be motivated to keep looking. But if

18 Duckworth, *Grit, 294.*

you think there is no point, you will almost certainly give up, guaranteeing you won't find a way.

Exciting new work is being done with children to help them see their learning as a process that can improve with hard work, as opposed to the demotivating idea that you are either smart or not. Believing you can improve and become more intelligent is called a "growth mindset." People with a growth mindset can change their beliefs. It is easier when we are young, but we never lose that ability. The science around neuroplasticity is exciting.

If any of the negative mindsets we addressed in this chapter are holding you back, then invest in yourself. If you find you have deep-seated issues that are causing the manifestations of toxic insecurity and preventing you from leaning into creative insecurity, be humble enough to ask for an expert's assistance in helping you grow through it. You are worth it. The world needs the best version of you.

CHAPTER 9

When Being First Is More Important Than Being Right

Being first with an idea is more important than being right. You are never right at first anyway; you become right through iteration. People look at me funny when I say this. They think, "Wait a minute, I want to be right." But it's impossible to be right before you experiment. You only become right through an iterative process. You will make many mistakes at this phase, so remain humble and adaptable. Voraciously consume data and avoid getting too attached to your ideas. Creators sometimes get superstitious about changing their drafts, which gets them in trouble.[1] As you are iterating, hold each idea loosely and explore multiple paths like you are scouting a reconnaissance mission before committing to a plan.

Being first means that you are also "only," which, by default, also makes you the best. Being first creates a monopoly of one, making it difficult for competitors to catch up because when they copycat you, you have already moved forward. It's a difficult gap to close. Sometimes, you keep looking

1 Rubin, *The Creative Act, 243.*

over your shoulder for the competition to arrive, and they never do. Our Central Admixture Pharmacy Services (CAPS) still has no meaningful competition.

I have been called a cheetah, which means I wait and watch, then strike fast when I see an opening. If conditions change, I abandon the original target quickly or bank hard into a pivot.

I often see talented entrepreneurs mapping elaborate business plans with complicated projection models. The first thing I ask is to see the assumptions. Why? Because nobody knows at that stage, and I want to get a feel for how good their instincts are. Sometimes, they are wildly off at that phase because they don't know what they don't know. Rather than trying to get the projections right, begin testing your assumptions with real people in the real world. Get out there and listen to prospective customers. Run a small test with a minimum viable product (MVP) and see what happens.[2] You will learn more by immersing yourself in the market than from the world's best research. Iterating is experimental, and failure is the best teacher there is. Keep your initial spreadsheets simple.

By running experiments, you can turn your assumptions into knowledge. Do so by rigorously comparing your hypotheses to what you learned. Too many founding teams make the mistake of assuming their guesses are facts.

Still, don't worry too much about competition, because the adage about a rising tide raising all boats is true. The high-tech home healthcare industry has never stopped growing.

---

2 Ries, *The Lean Startup*

Caremark continued to innovate, and fifty years later, the competition is still trying to catch the leader.

WHAT IF YOU ARE NOT THE FIRST MOVER?

And what if the competition got there first? Don't despair. Just be the first *to do it right.* History is full of first-to-market tech companies that don't exist today. They were overtaken by competitors who were the first to *do it right.* A person with a contrarian vision will always ask, "How could this have gone better?"

A great example is that the iPod was not the first portable music player. Others had been working on this technology, but Apple was the first to do it right.

One potential vulnerability of first movers is that they can become entrenched in their original way of approaching the market. They stop learning. They do not keep asking, "What am I missing?" They block new data. They don't iterate. They think they have it all figured out. Indeed, although being first to market should provide an enormous boost, academic research is mixed and does not support an overall first-mover advantage. It can and should be a big boost, but too many early entrants fall short because they do not continue to evolve when a shift occurs. If you have an early advantage, beware of hubris, which can cause you to squander the lead. People can fall hard when toxic insecurity makes them unwilling to look at all the data. They have closed minds and stop taking in information. They get attached to having it their way. They can't get out of their own head and be objective. An early lead should be a tremendous boon, so if you waste an early lead, then shame on you.

Because of your competitors' hubris, you can still take over the market, even if you are not first. If someone else was on the right track with an early idea, watch their mistakes and then pounce with a significant improvement. Research shows that if you swoop in and buck the trend in an entrenched market, you will be more likely to survive, receive funding, and go public than the first mover.[3]

How big should the increase be? In *Zero to One*, Peter Thiel says that if you want to overtake the leader, technological advancements should be ten times better.[4] CardioNet was an example of that. The Holter Monitor already tracked patients at home, but CardioNet was a step-function improvement over the competition. Be first to do it right, and do it in a big way.

TIMING

Some might call it luck, serendipity, or vision, but timing was a factor in the success of all my companies in terms of getting ahead of the wave. Everything became harder and more expensive for later entrants.

That is what a cheetah does: times the attack. Cheetahs have one of the highest success rates of all apex predators in the wild because of their exceptional speed. In the next section, we will discuss when timing favors a more methodi-

3 Grant, *Originals, 106.*
4 Thiel, *Zero to One, 48.*

cal approach, but if you see an opportunity expiring, it pays to be swift.

Another part of my success has come from playing a numbers game. I have constantly incubated new ideas and given them a space to sprout. If a seed germinates, I nurture it for a while, but if it withers, I abandon it quickly and move on to the growers. A few ideas will get past the first phase, but most won't.

Another aspect of timing is that sometimes you can find a climate that others deem unfavorable and turn it to your advantage by being a contrarian. For example, we had planned a road show to take CardioNet public in the summer of 2008. The markets crashed just as we entered that phase, but I convinced our team to proceed despite what was happening. When we showed up to meet with potential investors, they invariably said, "Why are you here? Do you know what a disaster the markets are going through?"

I said, "Well, I'm here for two reasons. Number one, I had no trouble getting an audience with you. There's nobody else waiting in line to see you. And number two, I've got a fantastic company that I need money for, and I'm not price sensitive."

So, we turned it into an advantage. We didn't give up and got our money.

AN EXAMPLE OF ITERATION—IV SOLUTIONS

When I started Caremark, it began around a single use case in IV solutions for total parenteral nutrition (TPN). By the time CVS bought the company, Caremark had created and led an entire category: high-tech home healthcare. How did this company go from a fledgling startup to an industry giant? Iteration.

Here are a few highlights to give an idea of the path, experiments, and pivots along the way. (Some of these innovations happened with Caremark and some were with our Central Admixture Pharmacy Services (CAPS):

- We started by convincing the wonderful Cleveland Clinic to take a chance on our product.
- We cajoled insurance carriers into paying for it. Once we had a template, others followed.
- We relied on Lily Mae Pledger and others as an example. First, we had to teach her how to compound solutions. This was a classic "minimum viable product," where we didn't wait to have the final process worked out. We moved ahead with what we could do most easily.
- We hired nurses and implemented countless processes to handle scheduling.
- We purchased McGaw, whose stellar reputation and distribution channels opened doors for us. We got around the contracts by introducing a "premix" through our central admixture pharmacy service (CAPS).
- To scale up, we built seventy central pharmacies nationwide with state-of-the-art cleanroom technologies.

- We created distribution systems to take orders and deliver the solutions to hospitals and patients directly.
- McGaw improved on the bag by using an inert material that would not leach into the patient's body or the environment.
- All along the way, we obtained regulatory and reimbursement approvals, raised capital, and managed investor relations.

These are just the highlights, which are oversimplifications, but the point is that each of these areas needed competent people who could build the processes from scratch. Then those processes needed iteration. Every time we tried something new, we had to experiment with what would work and improve until we dialed it in. To make this happen, we hired the best people we could recruit.

We made similar leaps with CardioNet, starting with an idea, validating that idea, and then learning we had to create a cell phone to do what we envisioned. We partnered with Qualcomm to build the hardware, and we hired a development team to write the software.

In the middle of growth, September 11, 2001, happened. This national tragedy meant we couldn't get funding as soon as needed. We had to lay off much of our workforce until the country stabilized. Meanwhile, we learned we'd have to locate our centralized monitoring facility to Philadelphia because of an obscure law change and our creative workaround.

In Philadelphia, we hired a team of technicians to do the monitoring. We had targeted the product launch, but our project manager, Teri Louden, rightly realized we had better test the product in the real world. The first patients showed us the bugs. One example: the monitor beeped all night, keeping patients awake. Can you imagine how much reputation we would have burned through with our cardiologists if their patients had complained about this? It could have undone us. We chose to delay the release for another six months.

When we finally launched the product, it worked beautifully. After building sufficient market share, we resolved to take the company public. By now, it was 2008. The markets crashed at what most people thought was the worst possible time for our IPO. But it wasn't. We made lemonade, using the lull to get appointments, build our book, and secure the investment we needed. Three months after our IPO, we did a secondary offering at a billion-dollar valuation.

And in a personal twist of fate, I have recently met with a cardiologist. He didn't know my background, and after examining me, he said, "…So, we'll put you on a CardioNet monitor to see what's happening." I became the recipient of my own product!

What I have just described is an example of a real company engaging in what is now known as "validated learning," according to the Lean Startup model pioneered by Eric Ries.[5]

---

5 Eric Ries, *The Lean Startup: How Today's Entrepreneurs Use Continuous Innovation to Create Radically Successful Businesses, Read by the author, (New York: Random House, 2011), Audible audio edition, 8 hr., 38 min.*

FAILING FAST—A NUMBERS GAME

Talking about failure has become something of a cottage industry, with the mantra "fail fast/fail often" becoming almost cliché in Silicon Valley. I see failure as a numbers game. One of my colleagues observed that in the time we've worked together, I have iterated through countless ideas and potential partnerships, with only a tiny handful making the cut for me to invest in or to mentor long-term. She likens it to catching lightning in a bottle.

This colleague also observed that I go through many trials to make all the mistakes quickly. "By the time he hits it," she said, "he has worked out all the bugs." She said this works because of, "Speed, decisiveness, and a willingness to be influenced by data. It requires personal flexibility."

In *Grit*, Angela Duckworth shares how experienced newspaper cartoonists will have a rejection rate north of 90 percent.[6] That seems about right; it's similar to my hit rate for big ideas or partnerships. I will pursue many but will ultimately abandon most. I've had plenty of ventures that never caught fire and a small handful that really made it. You can consider the ones that fizzled as failures, but I don't look at it that way. They were just part of the numbers game required to learn how to have a massive success.

Despite recent champions of embracing failure, most organizations are not very good at it. In an article by *Harvard Business Review* entitled "Failing by Design," author Rita McGrath asked leaders how effective their organizations were

6 Duckworth, *Grit, 69.*

at learning from failure on a scale of one to ten. They generally responded with a sheepish "one or two."[7] Thus, most organizations need help embracing failure or learning from it. The ones that are good at this type of learning—the exceptions—will distinguish themselves ahead of the pack. For example, one hallmark of *Built to Last* companies is that they "try a lot of stuff and keep what works."[8]

Here is another example of the numbers game. Can you guess what factor best predicts which composers will produce works considered masterpieces? It is not the composer's age, whether they were considered a prodigy, or other educational factors. It was how prolific they were. Those with the most masterpieces also had the highest number of works overall—most of which were unremarkable. Then, they composed a few shining, immortal pieces.

The London Philharmonic Orchestra listed the fifty greatest pieces of classical music: Mozart had six pieces, Beethoven five, and Bach three. To produce these masterworks, Mozart produced more than 600 pieces in his short lifetime, Beethoven wrote 650, and Bach wrote over 1000. This trend held in a study of over 15,000 masterworks—the more a composer produced, the greater the odds they would make a profound musical contribution. Similar statistics hold for Picasso and Shakespeare.[9] If you want to be original, "the most important possible thing you could do," says Ira Glass,

7 Rita McGrath, "Failing by Design," *Harvard Business Review*, April 2011, https://hbr.org/2011/04/failing-by-design.

8 Jim Collins and Jerry I. Porras, *Built to Last, (New York: Harper Business, 2002), 140.*

9 Grant, *Originals*, 36.

the producer of *This American Life*, "is do a lot of work. Do a huge volume of work."[10]

Here is my takeaway in business: if you want to land a big success, run a lot of experiments, and iterate quickly. Experiments are not failures if you learn something from them.

Before we flesh out what iterating looks like, however, I need to put in a word of caution about how I define embracing failure. Failure is productive when you do it early, keep it contained, and recover quickly. I'm not advising anyone to make catastrophic mistakes that end businesses and careers. You can avoid the trauma and financial ruin from big collapses if you are humble, open to data, and adaptable. I have never had a company go bankrupt, and I avoid big gambles. We will discuss mitigating risk further in Chapter 11.

EACH ITERATION GETS YOU CLOSER TO YOUR ECONOMIC DRIVERS

Iterating is the way you figure out the big and small details of your product and market positioning. It's also how you figure out your business's economic drivers. When I started, I had an ambitious but vague vision of wanting to make a difference by helping to keep people out of hospitals. With each new product development, Caremark eventually landed on our overarching concept. We were the leader in "high-tech home healthcare." Until that point, home healthcare was limited to the type of services where a nurse's aide might go to someone's home to help with bathing or wound care. It was a high touch, but low-tech industry. We changed that.

10 Grant, *Originals*, 36-37.

Our insight did not emerge overnight. Our progression followed a similar pattern to that of the *Good to Great* companies. It took years to develop what they call a "hedgehog concept." Here is their definition:

> A simple, crystalline concept that flows from deep understanding about the intersection of three circles: 1) what you are deeply passionate about, 2) what you can be the best in the world at, and 3) what best drives your economic or resource engine. Transformations from good to great come about by a series of good decisions made consistently with a Hedgehog Concept, supremely well executed, accumulating one upon another, over a long period.[11]

The term "hedgehog concept" comes from an essay by Isiah Berlin[12] in which he divides the world into hedgehogs and foxes, based on an ancient Greek parable. "The fox knows many things, but the hedgehog knows one big thing."[13]

Understanding the economic drivers will take time, but it's possible to accelerate learning if you create faster cycles and analyze the data. When something doesn't work, you can foster "intelligent failure," a term coined by Duke University's Sam Sitkin.[14]

---

11 Collins, *Good to Great*, 95.

12 Isiah Berlin, *The Hedgehog And the Fox, (UK: Weidenfeld & Nicholson, 1953).*

13 Collins, *Good to Great*, 90.

14 Sitkin, S.B. "Learning Through Failure: The Strategy of Small Losses." *Research in Organizational Behavior* 14, (January 1, 1992): 231–66.

One of the best ways to objectively get feedback is split testing, often called A/B testing, because different options are labeled A or B. Once the facts come in, management teams evaluate the results objectively rather than falling prey to vanity metrics that play to what they want to be true rather than what the market says is true.

The process of stating hypotheses, testing, and iterating is called "validated learning," in what Eric Ries calls the "build, measure, learn" feedback loop. Each round of testing should become more efficient, with faster cycle times and increasingly insightful results. The phrase hyper-iteration is how I describe this process. Ries also recommends pre-scheduling periodic meetings to make "pivot or persevere" decisions.[15] Without regular reflection, inertia keeps an organization running on the same trajectory, even if that is not the best direction.

The more experience you bring, the smarter your experiments will be. You can start a business in an industry where you haven't logged many years, but it will be harder. It will take more time to build your market understanding. You will make more experiential mistakes, and it will take longer to zero in on your core ideas. So, if you take this path, ensure you have plenty of runway. You may last longer if you don't quit your day job for a while. You can also stick with it if you have passion and a sense of purpose beyond your own interests.

Another way to accelerate learning is to study the work of others. Do your homework so you know what is out there,

15 *The Lean Startup, Eric Ries, Audible version, Sep 13, 2011, Random House Audio. 8 hr., 38 m.*

because the last thing you want to do is think your idea is innovative only to find out somebody has already done it better.

The best artists and inventors iterate on other people's work. They riff covers of great songs or mimic better artists until they gain enough confidence to combine influences into something new. Malcom Gladwell uses the example of Jeff Buckley's version of "Hallelujah," which most people recognize. Yet, as Gladwell explains, it's not a cover of the original "Hallelujah" by Leonard Cohen but a cover of John Cale covering Cohen's version.[16]

Especially if you are new to an industry, finding a mentor with the right background can help you avoid obvious pitfalls, design intelligent experiments, and analyze the results.

SCALING IT AFTER VALIDATION—THE BELL COW EFFECT

After a series of failed experiments and iterations, a company gets to the point of not "if" it will be successful but "how." Then, it is time to scale. Growth falls into place from there.

We have referred to creating something that didn't exist before as going from "zero to one." Scaling is taking that validated concept from "one to two."

A practice that has helped me is one I call "the bell cow effect."

On a farm, the lead cow has a bell around its neck, and the rest follow the leader. Humans are not so different; we will follow a perceived leader too. To break into a new market,

16 Malcolm Gladwell, "Hallelujah," 7/28/2016, in *Revisionist History*, produced by Pushkin, podcast, 44:12 (excerpt begins at 25:33), https://www.pushkin.fm/podcasts/revisionist-history/hallelujah.

identify the best, most prestigious target or client you could land. Choose the most influential customer success and use that success as an example to show others.

The Cleveland Clinic was well-respected and we picked it as our bell cow because it was one of the best hospitals in the world. We landed Mayo as our second major account, and the rest flowed from there.

That is why I moved to Cleveland. I wanted to be close and work out all the bugs. There, we started with a single customer with a single employer and insurance provider. These were big fish: Ford Motor Company and Blue Cross Blue Shield of Ohio. They became bell cows for other providers to follow. We went after Mayo Clinic next. As soon as we had these hospitals on our roster, others fell into line.

Often, you won't go after your ideal target in the first round. It can make sense to experiment on a third or fourth-tier customer where you can make mistakes without burning much capital in the marketplace.

Another time I targeted a bell cow was when I set my sights on getting funding from Kleiner, Perkins, Caufield, and Byers. I knew that I would get much more than money from them. They would open doors that nobody else could. And they were too important a target to approach first. Instead, I knocked on the door of every VC fund where I could get an appointment and gave my pitch. By the time I got to Kleiner Perkins, I had heard all the questions and had answers prepared. They did open doors, both in the short term and for the rest of my career. When it came time to raise capital in the future, I could point to a track record of success.

I have another corollary to share here. One time, I worked with someone who got into some legal trouble. I told my friend, "I've learned that there are a few times in life when you want to buy the best and cry once." I told him he needed to find the very best attorney. "I don't care how much they cost," I said. "Hire that person to get you out of this mess."

He didn't take my advice. He hired a lousy lawyer and lost the case; it cost him dearly. He paid twice, and I'd be surprised if he didn't cry.

That doesn't mean you should overspend. It can pay to shop for savvy ways to get the best. I work with an exceptional mergers and acquisitions attorney who previously charged three times as much as his current rate when he was part of a fancy firm. Now, he works in his hometown under his own name and doesn't have to pay all the overhead to the brand-name senior partners. He is still expensive, but he is the best and a bargain at his current rates. There was a time in my career when paying for a well-respected brand might have made sense, but that would be wasteful now.

STARTING NEW CHAPTERS

Each new episode is a new chapter. If you run an experiment that fails, do you stomp away in frustration? That's okay for a minute, but what do you do the next day? How do you feel about beginning again? Do you feel deflated by having to start over, or can you muster excitement at a new beginning? If a product or venture fails, do you give up on your dream, or do you try something else? If you can get excited about experiment number 40 or experiment number 999, then you have learned to lean into the unknown. Creative insecurity stimulates you.

One person interviewed for this book said, "Jim brings love to the first step over and over. He brings love to the clean sheet of paper, and he will bring that consistently."

Love is an apt word—I do *love* this process.

After selling Caremark, I felt some trepidation, but after the second success, I was hooked on starting new companies. The more ventures I started, the more that process became a core competency. I love starting again. Every day I am alive is another blank page, another chance to run an experiment and to learn. I want to continue growing until I die. Every day, I want to learn something, and I want to make an impact.

There are two kinds of experience. Somebody can have thirty years of experience, which is one year repeated thirty times. Someone else can have thirty years of experience where they're growing and learning every year. So, thirty years later, they're nothing like the person they were before.

People often ask me: "Do you miss such-and and-such?" I say, "Stop. I don't miss anything. That's behind me." I'm not looking in the rearview mirror because that is not the direction I'm headed. When they ask, "Where's the best place you have ever lived?" I say, "It's here, where I'm living now."

I believe that God is love. What does God do but create? God urges His creations to grow and evolve. Participating in the creative process allows us to tap into forces beyond ourselves. When we do creative work in the service of God and others, we touch the divine.

CHAPTER 10

DON'T MARRY A MISTAKE

I had a sales manager named Carl Bussema early in my career, and one of his famous lines was, "Don't marry a mistake." That stuck with me over the years because it's amazing how, when we fall in love with an idea, we are so unwilling to let go of it in the face of evidence that says, "You're wrong. This is wrong."

There is a nuance here to understand. Not quitting is one thing. Knowing when to quit is something else. It's a paradox, meaning we must have the wisdom to embrace both ideas simultaneously.

The no-quit gene says, "I'm going to persevere until I'm successful." It means never giving up on yourself. The decision to know what and when to quit comes from positive insecurity. It comes from continually validating your approach with external data.

I have a sad example of a time when I decided to quit an idea that I had been excited to launch. I was working on a business concept that would treat a certain type of patient so they could be released from the hospital and thrive at home. A superb physician said, "I love what you're doing so much that I'm going become a volunteer for your company when I retire next year."

But what she said next was a kick in the gut: "In the meantime, however, I can't refer any patients to you."

I asked, "Why not?"

She said, "Because in our facility, the patients who would be released are more economical to treat. The funding they bring in is what pays for the extra costs of the ones who are not doing as well."

That was a sad deal because our product could have especially helped babies born prematurely—something that felt personal because I was a preemie. However, perverse funding incentives meant our business model was not viable. It caused me to say, "Guess what? This dog isn't going to hunt." I calculated the odds and believed they were unwinnable—you can't buck such an entrenched system. Getting in the middle of hospital economics is a risky proposition.

I ended up handing off the idea to someone who believed they could get it to work. Maybe they knew something I didn't.

Our first product all those years ago had worked with the Cleveland Clinic because they were losing so much money on TPN treatments, they were thrilled to hand those patients to us. Their losses just evaporated. In that case, funding issues worked in our favor because they had an incentive to get the expenses off their books, not an incentive to keep them.

Your business idea should not be a matter of "against all odds, no matter what." It's got to work in the real world.

When we started CardioNet, I would have been willing to throw in the towel at any point if I had become convinced we had reached the end of the road. But there was no end there. We found solutions to every obstacle. We never stopped growing until we sold the company, because every new phase brought back more validation.

It doesn't always go the way you want, however, and sometimes you've got to change course. Eric Ries, who wrote *The Lean Startup*, says that one of the hardest decisions any entrepreneur will face is whether to pivot or persevere. Ries urges founders to use the scientific method to state clear hypotheses about business models and product ideas and then test those hypotheses. It is a tremendous source of waste to create product features that don't add value to customers.

"There is no bigger destroyer of creative potential," Ries says, "than the misguided decision to persevere." He warns entrepreneurs against the danger of failing to implement hard decisions. "Companies that cannot bring themselves to pivot to a new direction on the basis of market response can get stuck in the land of the living dead, neither growing enough or dying, consuming resources and commitment from employees and other stakeholders but not moving ahead."[1]

Now, I want to share a more lighthearted example of when I changed direction in my personal life. When my kids were growing up, I argued with them when they wanted to get tattoos. I railed against the idea, calling people who get tattoos "losers" and using every persuasive argument I could think of to convince my kids they shouldn't get one.

1 *The Lean Startup, Eric Ries, Audible version, Sep 13, 2011, Random House Audio. Chapter 8.*

Guess what? Last year, I got my first tattoo. I realized that the landscape has changed. Tattoos do not carry the stigma they once did. It seemed like a fun thing to do, and so I got one. I called my kids and ate crow. We had a good laugh about it.

It is an example of how I take pride in being the kind of person who can change my mind if a better argument comes along. Even at this stage of my life, I never want to become rigid in my ideas. I want to continue expanding my mind with new points of view.

GOING FAST DOES NOT MEAN GOING RECKLESS

Even cheetahs, which have one of the highest success rates in the animal kingdom, only get dinner slightly more than half the time.

A cheetah is precise and does not waste motion on erratic tries with little chance of success. Part of the reason a cheetah has such a high kill rate is that they only expend energy on opportunities with a high probability of success. I run a lot of experiments, but I only plunk significant resources into a startup once it has reached a threshold of viability. Likewise, if you see a yellow flag, you've got to chase it down because it could turn into a red flag. People often overlook warning signs because they don't like what those signs could mean. Trust me, the consequences only worsen when you ignore unfavorable facts. It's essential to maintain rigor in running experiments and evaluate the data in an emotionally detached way. You can't fall so in love with your ideas that you become blind to the facts.

In short, going fast does not mean going reckless.

I became a helicopter pilot, which is a risky activity. I learned that there are old pilots and there are bold pilots, but there are no old, bold pilots. I once took Larry Watts up for a helicopter ride in Kauai, which is a place where a lot of helicopter accidents happen. Larry is not a big risk-taker either, and he observed many similarities to being a helicopter pilot and CEO. "Jim likes being in control," Larry said, "but he also does everything on the checklist. He is not willy-nilly about preparation in the slightest, either in business or in the helicopter."

You will save resources overall when you take the time to test your theories and collect market insights. You will be glad you trusted your instincts and chased down any yellow flags.

Good CEOs only take calculated risks after taking in ample information. They do not go to Las Vegas. If you were to survey the sixty CEOs funded by Kleiner Perkins when I was there, not one of them would go to Las Vegas and gamble. Not one of them. Yet, we were all willing to bet our whole careers on our companies. That is because we could control the odds, whereas the odds would always be against us in Vegas. These CEOs evaluate situations and get to a point where they can control enough of the variables that their risk is very low. They are managing situations within their skill sets. These were remarkably successful people who built companies whose names you would recognize.

Another example of managing risk comes from Alex Honnold, the free-solo climber who scaled El Capitan. "Preparation," he says, "Is what stops fear." He memorized all the hand and foot holds for all three thousand feet of his climbing route, likening it to the way a chess grand master can glance at a game in progress and memorize the position of all the pieces on the board.

When researchers did an fMRI on Honnold's brain, they saw that his amygdala responds differently to fear than most people's do. He attributes that to twenty-five years of training it, which rewires the brain. This phenomenon can also be seen in the brains of monks after years of repetitive meditation.

Honnold goes on to say, "The casual observer might think free soloing is all crazy and reckless. But you can't have a long career unless you spend a tremendous amount of time thinking about risk and minimizing it to ensure your own safety." By the time he's in the middle of a high-risk climb, he has already done the creative work to prepare, and he sticks to the plan.

"I don't want to be improvising. That would bring more uncertainty and risk into the equation." Honnold says.[2] His fMRI scans also illustrate how being prepared is one of the best ways to combat fear. Having a plan for every movement frees the mind to focus and not panic.

I have also taken some calculated risks. These include putting a second mortgage on my house to buy shares in Caremark and putting the seed capital into CAPS once I saw what a profitable business it would be.

Every one of my companies had two or three near-death experiences where I've had to wonder, "How am I going to

2 Harrell, "Life's Work, Alex Honnold."

manage my way out of this?" It was never a stroll in the park. But when you find yourself in a pickle, you find ways to claw your way through it. I've had enough insecurity to wake up at three o'clock every morning saying, "What did I miss? What did I not think about that's going to bite me in the butt?" Managing risk is identifying the issues early and getting ahead of them.

At least one study has found that the most successful businesspeople are not risk takers but are, instead, highly risk-averse.[3] They are the kind of people who get ulcers when there is too much risk for their comfort, and they take every precaution to reduce their exposure. Despite stereotypes in the popular culture of the daredevil entrepreneur, they are cautious until they have landed on the sure thing, and then they bet big. People likely have that image because of the dramatic stories of people who made it big after betting everything. Economist Scott Shane says that many entrepreneurs take plenty of risks, but those are generally the failed entrepreneurs. The problem with the gambler narrative is that the ones who didn't survive are forgotten. We never hear about them.[4]

Successful entrepreneurs do not take a "damn the torpedoes" approach by plunging headlong into danger, and they are not braver than other people. Instead, they are more analytical. Shane says they are more like apex predators in the

---

3 Michel Villette and Catherine Vuillermot, "From Predators to Icons, Exposing the Myth of the Business Hero," Translated by George Holoch (New York: Cornell University Press), 2009.

4 Gladwell, "The Sure Thing," quoting Scott Shane, *The Illusions of Entrepreneurship, (Yale University Press, 2008)*

natural world who look for the least possible risk while hunting.[5] Cheetah!

This perspective is validated by Jim Collins in *Great by Choice*, which we mentioned earlier in our section on creating systems for data. This book compared companies that thrived in uncertain times, which they called 10X companies because they were ten times better than comparison companies from the same industries that had lackluster performance. The study found that both groups of CEOs took bold risks, but the 10X leaders were hypervigilant, analyzed data, and mitigated risk. They exercised "productive paranoia." These companies prepared for the worst. CEOs of 10X companies ask this key question: "How much time do we have until our risk profile changes?"[6]

The 10X CEOs had another practice for taking risks, which the *Great by Choice* authors called "fire bullets, then cannonballs." The idea is that they first fired inconsequential shots and calibrated their aim accordingly. They ran small experiments and gathered data. Once they saw that they were consistently hitting the target, they channeled considerable resources. In other words, they shot a cannonball.[7]

This tracks my observation about how CEOs are not gamblers; they only take calculated risks when the odds are in their favor. They have confidence in themselves and their businesses, but this optimism is tempered by humility and

---

5 Gladwell, "The Sure Thing"
6 Collins, *Great by Choice*, 131.
7 Collins, *Great by Choice*, 113.

even a healthy dose of imposter syndrome that drives them to become better. They have a clear-eyed outlook toward risk.

When we are in the middle of calibrating, I might tell my team, "We're in the right ZIP code but not at the right house yet." We keep dialing it in until we confidently say, "We have arrived at the right house."

This is precisely what we did when we created the "Respect" video. I had a sense of what the research would say, but we still validated our idea with pharmacists. Once we got that far, we knew we had a winner, and we spent big on the video and event. That event was a cannonball, not a wild bet. It was not roulette.

When you take the time to analyze a situation and build a proper foundation you are going fast but not reckless. First, you prepare. Then you strike hard. You double down on your bets and cut spending entirely on other projects. Jim Collins says the purpose of budgeting is to determine which projects should be fully funded and which should not be funded at all.[8]

Sometimes, slow is fast. This means not seeking shortcuts but choosing the "long way," as Seth Godin calls it, "The shortcut that's sure to work, every time: Take the long way. Do the hard work, consistently and with generosity and transparency. And then you won't waste time doing it over."[9]

Once you have validated your idea, it may seem like it takes forever to get off the ground. That is, if you are building

---

8 Jim Collins, "How Do You Do 'Stop Doing,'" (jimcollins.com, 2017), transcript of audio, https://www.jimcollins.com/media_topics/StopDoing.html.

9 Seth Godin, *Seth's Blog, The Certain Shortcut*, https://seths.blog/2013/05/the-certain-shortcut/

a proper foundation. We took the long way when we built a cell phone to do what we needed from a heart monitor, relocated the monitoring center in Philadelphia, and hired a whole team.

Successful entrepreneurs lean into the thrill of pushing off from the dock but have enough humility to over-prepare for the risks. Explorers who make it back home first worry about all the ways they can die, and they run practice drills. They mitigate risks and leave some margin for error. They stay alert for changing conditions. If they see a storm rolling in, they activate contingency plans quickly.

THE PARADOX OF KNOWING AND NOT KNOWING

You become indefatigable about your big idea when you *know* you are right about it. But there is a flip side to that. "Knowing" has qualifications. I'll give you an example. When I started my company, I saw these patients at the Cleveland Clinic coming into the hospital and getting fed intravenously for two weeks and, going home and starving for weeks, and then coming back and being tethered to the hospital. I looked at that and said, "I can deliver what they need at home. I *know* that. And I also know people will want to do this on that basis."

On the other hand, you must ask questions and be insecure about what you don't know. There was so much we didn't know in the beginning about how it would all work. We had to figure out the "how" later.

If you have a flash of inspiration and you become convinced that it is right, that can be dangerous, because the moment most people utter the words, "I know," they stop asking questions. It's much better to say, "I have a hypothesis." I like to say, "I think I know." Then, you test the hypothesis. You start with assumptions and test whether they are right or wrong. Eventually, you become confident that your idea is on point. And *then*, you need to learn the how. That is where you must be indefatigable about the execution. You must be flexible in trying new approaches.

One pitfall for those blessed with exceptional intuitive gifts or contrarian vision is relying too much on their own ideas. If you are used to being right, that mindset can become a bad habit. You stop taking in all the data available to you. You stop listening to information contrary to your own opinion. You stop being flexible in the how. This is hubris. If you fall into this trap, your winning streak won't last. This adage applies to listening to your instincts: *trust, but verify.*

RIGOROUS, NOT RUTHLESS

Companies in the *Good to Great* study were rigorous in implementing their findings. That extends to making decisions about people. However, Collins and his team go on to differentiate between being rigorous and being ruthless. Don't use the guise of rigor to slash jobs for short-term gains. The right people are your most valuable asset, so first, make sure you don't have a fit issue. That person may simply be in the wrong seat on the bus. The bad apples, however, should be relieved of command. The longer you keep them, the more everybody in the company knows you're letting mediocrity take over.

I advise offering clear communications and expectations, then giving people a chance to improve. Do not hesitate when you need to have these conversations. Once you know what is needed, don't delay. Listen to your gut instincts, not your emotions, to guide these decisions. Ask yourself, *would I hire this person again*? If not, then a change is in order.

Letting the situation drag on will demoralize your team, undermine your credibility, and rob that person of the chance to move on. Every day they spend with you is a day they aren't working in another environment where their talents will be a better fit. Dragging it out robs a person of a part of their lives. *That* is ruthless, and it is self-serving because you didn't want to deal with uncomfortable emotions.

When you must have a conversation to deliver the news, never take more than ten minutes to do so. Your decision is made. Respectfully tell them the situation, thank them for their service, and don't let it drag out. It is both cruel and dishonest to let someone think it is a discussion and there may be some way to turn it around. Those conversations should have happened much earlier. Please do not make it death by a thousand cuts.

These moments are trying for everyone. They will test your resolve. They will test how indefatigable you are. You never want to feel you have gotten good at this part of the job. Times like these will test whether you have learned to say, "What you think of me is none of my business." If you terminate someone's employment, you already know that person will not like you.

If you can't make decisions like this, then your no-quit gene isn't what you thought it was. Get some support and do the hard thing. You will grow through the process, and you will be stronger afterward. Your organization will function better, and your life will improve once it is done. You will be amazed by how much better the work environment feels afterward. People will comment on how the energy is palpably better. If you dragged your feet, you will wonder why you didn't do it sooner.

WHAT SHOULD YOU QUIT?

In *The Dip*, Seth Godin cites Vince Lombardi's famous quote, "Winners never quit, and quitters never win." Godin then follows this by countering, "This is bad advice. Winners quit all the time. They just quit the right stuff at the right time."[10]

Most of us are good at creating to-do lists. When was the last time you made a "stop-doing" list?[11]

EXIT WHEN YOU REACH THE END OF THE ROAD

Exit if your assumptions are incorrect to the point that the business model is not viable. If you reach the end of a road,

---

10 Seth Godin, *The Dip: A Little Book that Teaches You When to Quit (and When to Stick)*, (Audible Studios, 2007), Audible Audiobook edition. 1 hr., 32 min.

11 Jim Collins, "How Do You Do 'Stop Doing,'" (jimcollins.com, 2017), transcript of audio, https://www.jimcollins.com/media_topics/StopDoing.html.

let go and start down a new path. Don't destroy yourself and others by hanging on too long.

Why did the United States stay in Vietnam long after it was clear we should exit? Pride. I once saw that pride in real time when I attended a conference for CEOs. Robert McNamara, the Secretary of Defense during Vietnam, was invited to speak. He droned on for two hours trying to justify his actions in Vietnam. He had such arrogance that he did not prepare a talk that would be of value to the room; it seemed to me that he only wanted to soapbox his ego. Some attendees couldn't stomach it and left before he finished.

I want to point out again how different Jay Leno was when he emceed our event and played the "Respect" video compared to how McNamara acted. Leno was a star but had enough humility to make our event about the audience. McNamara was only speaking for himself.

EXIT WHEN MARKET FORCES BECOME UNFAVORABLE

At times in the healthcare world, the entire industry's payment models or other dynamics were changing. Regulations can upend an industry's economics. I could see what was coming over the horizon and that it was time to get out.

EXIT WHEN YOUR SKILLSET IS NOT A GOOD MATCH FOR THE NEXT PHASE

Regarding this one, I have learned that my strengths lie in the startup phase. I know that I love the blank page, new beginnings, and solving problems. I don't love politics and am not very good at that part of the business. There comes a point in any company's growth when politics start taking too much of the day for my liking. I exit when I know other people will be better at doing the job ahead than I can be. I know they'll go on to build the company bigger and bigger. The simple reason I started fourteen companies instead of staying with one forever is that I hate politics. Some founders have the skills and inclination to grow their companies indefinitely. That just wasn't me.

It is also important to realize that the economics are very different when a business reaches scale, and the industry matures. Competition sets in, margins erode, and it takes a very different type of business to succeed in that environment. It made sense for CVS to buy Caremark and integrate it into CVS's enormous distribution channels, pharmacy network, and nursing infrastructure. They have a model that makes up for lower margins with high volume.

EXIT WHEN THE SCHLEP-TO-THRILL FACTOR IS NOT THERE ANYMORE

I have a friend who is a skier. He said, "You know, Jim, I decided to stop skiing." I was surprised, and he explained, "Well, the schlep-to-thrill factor is not there anymore. I do all the schlepping: I get all my gear loaded up. I put it in the car. I drive to the mountain. I put on my boots. I pull out my skis. I schlep to the top of the mountain. Then I ski down the hill for two minutes and start over again. There's too much schlepping and not enough thrill."

After hearing that, you wouldn't believe how many times per day I look at a situation that I'm confronted with and say, you know, the schlep-to-thrill factor is not there. The effort is no longer worth the reward.

That's one reason it's so essential to pick a billion-dollar idea. The outcome is worth sticking with it. Start a business you are personally passionate about and that will bless others. These factors greatly increase the thrill factor and will make you indefatigable. It will be hard work, but it will be fun.

If you specialize in early-stage ventures, there will come a time in your business growth when the schlep-to-thrill factor is no longer there. That's how you know it's time to exit.

CHAPTER 11

Humility Is the Bedrock

Throughout my healthcare career, I witnessed three companies that each could have been so much more profitable and successful if their leaders had set their egos aside. The three were Baxter, Abbott, and American Hospital Supply. They were situated within twenty miles of each other, all in the north Chicago area. Their executives all belonged to the same golf clubs, ran in the same social circles, and they enjoyed harumphing about how much better they were than the others.

The only thing these companies had in common was that they each owned IV solution companies. Since there were three companies, this space was an oligopoly which are historically extraordinarily profitable. But in this case, they destroyed their profits in a race to the bottom because they wanted to eke out more market share than the others, so they kept driving the prices down. Rather than concede some market share but keep their profits, they would each do price cuts until none were making much money on this business. Worse, their positions never really changed compared to the others. They destroyed their self-interest by letting their country-club egos run the show.

CONFIDENT HUMILITY

Humility enhances vision and the no-quit gene. Humility keeps these other traits in the Contrarian's Trifecta from running amok, like we saw in the example above. Humility is the bedrock of the Contrarian's Trifecta. Humility provides an environment where creative insecurity can thrive and where you enjoy the thrill of new beginnings while staying alive. Without humility, your hard work, your dreams, and your desire to serve the world will be for naught. Trust me on this.

We live in a culture that feeds you narcissistic lies that prop up the ego. Don't get sucked in by believing those lies. Learn to govern yourself, because hubris is the great undoer.

This chapter shows what humility looks like in authentic leadership. Models are rarer in the public eye, but if you have seen an outstanding organization firsthand with a mission of service and engaged staff, you will likely find humility baked into its culture.

Have you ever had the privilege of working with a leader who exemplifies humility? Pause for a moment to consider what that was like. What did you enjoy and admire? What did that style of leadership do for others on the team?

As my co-author and I considered these examples, she shared the following experience from her career:

> Before I became a full-time writer, I worked as a vice president at a state college. My boss, the president, was an extraordinary woman named Collette Mercier. She had a fierce will and exceptionally high standards. I loved working for her because

she drove the entire institution to do great things and brought out the best in her team. She was a model of poise and self-control but was humble too. She was the kind of person who never walked past a piece of trash on campus without picking it up, even if it meant walking onto the grass in her heels.

One year, we nominated her for a statewide award called "Women to Watch," which she received. She reluctantly accepted because we convinced her it would be good publicity for the college. We got invited to a fancy award luncheon at the Grand America Hotel. The event planners had previously interviewed all the women and created videos about them. These were impressive women, and it was fun to learn about their accomplishments. When Collette came on, I felt pride in seeing how well she represented us. Then I noticed something. She never once talked about herself in that video. Not once. She spoke of the college's mission, how we partnered with local employers, and helped students reach their potential. I don't recall her using the word "I." It wasn't false modesty either. That's just how she was—all the time.

Had someone interviewed me in that environment, would I have set my ego aside and only spoke for the institution? Probably not. Her high

> leadership standards set the bar for who I want to become. I'm still working toward that standard and wonder if I will ever get there. But I want to.

If you have some work to do, you're in good company. Most of us must practice keeping our egos in check throughout life. We cannot let our guard down.

Do you *want* to embrace humility?

If you do, there is hope. Humility starts with a desire to be humble. There is a class of people who will never change because their egotistical behaviors make them feel powerful. They are convinced they are right. They fear insecurity, so they overcorrect. Their big egos and fragility both stem from fear.

Beware of leaders who are paranoid someone else might show them up. Beware of anyone who must be the smartest person in the room. These people have an attitude of "seldom wrong, never in doubt," and they miss much because they do not listen. They shut out data that might prove them wrong. Their blind spots are enormous because they're too scared to look around.

A great line from the song "If I Were a Rich Man" from *Fiddler on the Roof* says, "When you're rich, they think you really know." What a bunch of BS. People ascribe all this genius to wealth that doesn't exist. What's worse is when *you* think you really know.

Humility will enable you to be insecure about what you don't know. Only those with enough faith can step into the realm of uncertain outcomes. They have enough confidence to believe they can learn and adapt to unknown situations.

Healthcare today is a fascinating study as big tech companies come into the space, confident they can fix problems. They swagger in, hire brilliant healthcare professionals, and then disregard their insights because the answers are too complex for their liking. Hubris doomed the Buffet-Bezos-Dimon venture to fail. I suspect that their success in their respective areas made them overlook their ignorance regarding healthcare. It's a great irony that Warren Buffet's famous advice is to stick within your circle of competence, yet he broke his own rule by charging into this industry.

YOU CONTINUE TO BE SUCCESSFUL AS LONG AS YOU CONTINUE TO BE HUMBLE

If you are early in your career, you may eagerly soak in as much as you can learn. That is the right attitude and one that will endear you to others. Humility will keep you flexible, and flexibility is a hallmark of youth.

If you are talented, you will bump into ego on your journey. Count on it. Peter Drucker said, "Strong people always have strong weaknesses too."[1] That includes a propensity toward hubris.

If you are successful, you can only keep growing if you remain humble. As soon as you let ego, entitlement, and narcissism take hold, you'll slide backward. As soon as you become rigid, you'll be old and obsolete (regardless of your age).

---

1 Quote attributed to Peter Drucker on quoteinvestigator.com. Peter Drucker, *The Effective Executive, (New York: Harper & Row, hardcover edition), 72.*

Leaders I mentor often express this concern, *If I encounter success, how do I keep my ego in check? How do I have big dreams but a small ego?*

I once watched a star who rose through the leadership ranks quickly, jumping too many levels too soon, and he developed a larger-than-life personality. I once suggested I didn't think his board would go along with a plan he presented to me, and he responded, "You don't know who you're talking to." That implied he thought he could do whatever he wanted. His board did not go along with his idea.

In retrospect, I think he suffered from toxic insecurity because he hadn't matured into his rank. He was like a cottonwood tree that grows fast but cracks in a heavy wind. He compensated with hubris. The industry changed when Diagnosis Related Groups came along in an attempt to control costs, and his growth rate evaporated. His ego would not allow him to accept this new reality. It was tragic to watch what happened next because he had shown so much promise, but his career became unhinged. He ultimately sold the company to a competitor in what is known as a bear hug, and Wall Street threw up all over the idea. The company lost its autonomy. His insecurities fed a sad end to the great company that once was. It was a real shame.

In contrast, I had the privilege of working with Vernon Loucks, who became the CEO of Baxter and eventually acquired Caremark. Loucks had grown up cutting the grass of Bill Graham, the prior CEO of Baxter. He got a Harvard MBA, and Graham eventually turned the company over to Loucks. Loucks had come from an affluent family and earned a string of successes a mile long, but he never lost his humility. That was his way of being all the time.

Humility is not pretending; it's practicing. Practice the disciplines of humility until they become habits.

HUMILITY IS A CHOICE

Every person is born with both the seeds of ego and humility. Ego, like laziness, comes naturally. We must all train humility like any other muscle or difficult skill. Learning it can be uncomfortable, but that's how we grow. The good news is that humility is not some inborn talent that some are gifted with, and others are not.

Make a conscious choice to adopt these disciplines to keep your ego in check and develop your humility.

I have identified three disciplines of humility:

1. Flexibility
2. Gratitude
3. Love

DISCIPLINE #1: FLEXIBILITY

Flexibility is a function of humility because you are curious about what you do not know and are willing to adapt. Curiosity is cousin to flexibility, motivating us to override fear and venture into the unknown.

You can train yourself to remain flexible in your ideologies and examine your prejudices. One stunning example comes from Daryl Davis, a black musician who spends time with

Ku Klux Klan members and has helped many reexamine their beliefs. He recalls wondering as a child, "How can you hate me when you don't even know me?"[2] When he spent time with one KKK district leader, Davis listened to the man. He then helped him to examine his belief that black people are more violent by pointing out the similarly absurd premise that most serial killers are white. Neither argument holds water. Thus, Davis started a series of conversations that led to friendship. This approach eventually turned the man's beliefs upside down, and he left the Klan a few months later. Davis claims to have helped some two hundred white supremacists leave extremist groups. He did it by forming a relationship with people who couldn't have seemed more different. Today, he has a collection of KKK robes and hoods given to him by people who abandoned the Klan.[3] The world has changed a lot since the Klan began. If Klan members can change their minds, so can you.

What you thought was true yesterday may not be true today. Are you curious about those changes? Are you willing to update your facts?

Adaptation is how a species survives. It takes humility to part with an idea and jump onto a better one. Doing so is easier after you examine both sides of an argument with equal fervor.

When you find yourself resisting, feeling fearful, or being defensive, note it, and make a course correction. Practice say-

---

2 Nicholas Krostof, "How Can You Hate Me When You Don't Even Know Me?" op-ed, *New York Times*, June 26, 2021, https://www.nytimes.com/2021/06/26/opinion/racism-politics-daryl-davis.html.

3 Grant, *Think Again, 140.*

ing, "tell me more" and the related phrases from this book. Pay attention to how you are feeling in your body. You may not realize that your fight-or-flight instinct has engaged. You can overcome it with awareness. Breathing will calm your pulse and will return oxygen to your brain. Asking questions will trigger curiosity and activate the thinking brain.

Practicing humility takes patience, but even small changes are noticeable to others. In this way, you will be like a flexible palm tree and not a brittle cottonwood. A palm tree can survive a hurricane because it bends without snapping.

Another cousin to flexibility is serendipity, which is one of my favorite words. I have friends who plan trips down to the minute, and they have a great time. I do just the opposite. I get on a plane, go somewhere, and let it happen. Serendipity has given me some marvelous memories. There is a certain hubris in needing to control. It's an illusion anyway, so why not have fun and go with the flow?

And don't underestimate the power of luck. Luck is what happens when preparation meets opportunity, as the Roman philosopher Seneca said. Be open to it. Be grateful for it. And be flexible enough to change your plans when it comes along. Studies have shown that companies that thrive do not have more good luck than their counterparts, they're just better at managing risk and taking advantage of good luck. They are known for turning unfortunate circumstances into opportunities.[4] Luck favors the prepared.[5]

---

4 Collins, *Great by Choice, 191.*

5 Louis Pasteur said, "Chance favors the prepared mind." Later, the character Edna Mode from *The Incredibles movie said, "Luck favors the prepared."*

A sure way to be *unhappy* is to be rigid about your expectations. Expectations are the precursor to disappointment. Serendipity is the opposite—delighting in the unexpected. Failure is also our greatest teacher, humbling us to see what we resisted before. Humility makes us coachable, teachable, and ready to change. Failure prepares us to try something new, creating flexibility where we previously fought it. That is why breakthroughs often happen after the dark night of the soul.

Tips for practicing flexibility:

- Look for serendipity when you already have other plans.
- Look for growth after mistakes. How did you change? What breakthroughs happened because of failure?
- Reframe failure as a positive when you process events in retrospect. This will help you have a more flexible, resilient mindset when you experience speed bumps in the future.

DISCIPLINE #2: GRATITUDE

Another discipline of humility is gratitude. Being grateful rather than entitled bears so many benefits that I'm sure you already know.

Here is how I cultivate this attitude. I have a practice of writing a gratitude journal each morning. In it, I list people I am grateful for by name. Currently, this list has thirty-eight names on it.

This practice is a form of prayer for me and sets an intention for my day that comes from a place of abundant gratitude. It sets the tone for my work.

At the close of each day, I pause and think, "Was this a plus day or a minus day?" I can't remember the last time I had a minus day. I am grateful for them all.

DISCIPLINE #3: LOVE

The final and most important discipline of humility (and life) is love. When you love others, you will serve and respect them. You will be unselfish about your work, and your ego will naturally stay in check. It begins with loving yourself.

Love is the most vital force in the universe and should underscore everything we do. When we come at our work from a place of love, things have a way of working out. The ego has an easier time sitting in the corner. Why? Because love takes up all the space. There is little room for ego if your heart is bursting with love. You will also be more motivated to persevere in your work when you are doing it from a place of service. The no-quit gene and humility strengthen each other.

How can you increase a desire to serve? When proceeding with a project or an action, ask yourself your motive. Are you doing it for yourself, for credit, for self-importance, for financial rewards, or are you doing it for a cause?

Humility comes more naturally when you're devoted to a cause instead of being devoted to yourself. If you're doing it for yourself, work on an honest attitude adjustment. You can't fake this. When you're genuinely devoted to serving others, the no-quit gene follows.

HUMBLE PEOPLE COMMUNICATE USING THE "YOU-POINT-OF-VIEW"

In every interaction with others and in every communication, convey respect. Respect comes from a place of love. That was the message of our video to the pharmacists, and it has become a guiding principle of my life. When we elevated Lily Mae Pledger in the eyes of doctors, we showed her with dignity. We respected that she was capable, motivated, and worthy of living a fulfilling life outside the hospital.

I call this the "you-point-of-view."[6] In every conversation, talk "to" someone, never "at" someone. Don't frame your arguments as you see them, first see how others think of the situation.

I want to understand what will motivate you. I want to understand what will cause you to want to make a difference. I never want to point a finger at you; the idea is to work together to solve problems.

Here is another story about service. When awareness of AIDS first swept through the United States, there was widespread panic. Patients weren't being treated in the hospital because no one knew what to do. Doctors dressed in what looked like moonwalk suits, and some caregivers refused to enter the home of a patient with AIDS.

Nothing was working for these patients at the time. They would go into an intensive care unit until their insurance coverage ran out and then would be sent home. It was horrible.

---

6 I originally learned the "you-point-of-view" as part of my undergraduate business degree from San Diego State University. I wish to give credit, but sadly, I no longer recall which course I got this idea from or the professor's name.

We set about finding ways to help these patients at home. The first thing we had to do was scrutinize the known facts. We reached out to people at the CDC who were helpful, and we wrote up something similar to blood-borne hepatitis protocols. Then we ran it past them, asking, "Do you think this is safe enough?" The CDC worked with us and said, "Yeah, they should be fine."

We did training programs with our drivers and nurses about handling sharps (needles) and what to do if there was a needle stick. Incidentally, that never ended up happening.

Meanwhile, we got a call from MD Anderson, the prestigious hospital for cancer patients I mentioned earlier. They asked if we worked with AIDS patients. We said, "Oh yes, we do. Why do you ask?"

They said they were now treating patients with AIDS, but they ran into an issue with our competitor, who currently had the contract. This competitor refused to enter the home to train patients to administer their IV solutions. Their delivery people just dropped supplies on the porch, rang the doorbell, and ran.

We were happy to take that business back from our competitor and, more importantly, to treat these patients with dignity and respect during a terrible time.

One of our drivers became friends with a patient. He usually delivered on Monday but had to come back on Friday, only to find that the person had died. He talked with the patient's family about his experience. He was so moved that he went back to college and came to work in our finance department because he wanted to make a career in healthcare.

We had patients dying in the arms of our employees. I don't mean that as hyperbole; that did happen. Our nurses offered genuine compassion to patients cut off from the outside world.

Meanwhile, we had a longstanding advertising contract for the back page of a hospital magazine. An agency had been managing it for us, and they had been running the same tired, boring ad forever. Larry Watts brought it to me and asked what I thought.

I pretended to barf on it. Larry didn't usually write the ads, but he decided to try something bold with this one.

He staged a photo shoot showing a competitor's delivery outside on a front porch getting wet in the rain. Deborah Meyers went out and took the photo. The headline ran something like, "The cold reality behind warm promises about patient care." The copy explained that competitors were unwilling to help these struggling, weak patients who were homebound.

We usually did not run such pointed ads, but Larry felt compelled to call them out on this one. He predicted it would be controversial, so he brought it to me. He asked my opinion, and I said, "I love this."

He asked, "Should we show it around?"

I said, "I don't understand, Larry. If I like it and you like it, why do we care what anyone else thinks?"

Larry said, "Well, that may be true for you, but I have to live here." So, he did show it around. Our colleagues thought it was the greatest thing, and we ran it. Yes, we heard about it from our competitors, but it became such a scandal that our competitors changed their policy.

When Larry reflected on it, he said, "If you just sit around being tasteful, no one will notice you. You have to show something that people care about, and that answers a real problem."

We became the treatment option of first resort for AIDS patients throughout the United States, especially in San Francisco, which was ground zero for that epidemic. We said, "We're going to embrace these patients. We will not run away from them." That was the hallmark of our company.

Another example of the "you-point-of-view" comes from Cleveland Clinic, which had a cultural sea change to become a patient-centric organization. They improved their food and did away with visiting hours, thereby encouraging families to visit whenever they could. Another powerful signal was reassigning the reserved parking spaces near the front of buildings to patients, not doctors. One physician complained, "What is this, patients first and doctors last?" *Exactly.*[7]

The "you-point-of-view" is a learned behavior. Create an environment where everyone values questions and feels empowered to speak. Value the best ideas, not tenure or authority. This is about listening, caring, and developing empathy.

---

7 Cosgrove, *The Cleveland Clinic Way, 112-113*

CHAPTER 12

Hubris Is the Great Undoer

A while back, I went to an event for a nonprofit cause I care about. On that trip, I met the leader and came away knowing we would not work together.

First, I have to say that when there is a red-carpet event with cameras flashing and people dripping with diamonds, that is not where you want to be. This leader struck me as a larger-than-life character with an ego to match. The more I learned afterward, the more I believe my initial assessment to be correct. Then, a year or so after we met, reports of misconduct surfaced from credible sources. They were pretty damning and very sad. As I speculate about what happened, it seems to me that this person got caught up in a God complex, believing the mission to be so important that the ethical boundaries binding mere mortals did not apply. That sort of behavior has a way of catching up with you.

I wish I could say this case was rare, but hubris is the rule; humility is the exception. Humility underpins everything we have talked about in this book. Hubris can undo it.

Indefatigability without humility can turn someone into a raving zealot or the kind of person who will trample over others and justify it for the cause. Vision without humility can turn someone into a person caught up in grandiosity.

Ego can kill profitability and undo all your hard work. Examples of hubris are everywhere in the media and government these days. Our culture celebrates vanity while overlooking people with true character. It can seem like modesty goes unnoticed in a landscape where people are vying to build an audience. But in the long run, qualities related to humility do endear loyalty, foster long-term relationships, and build strong corporate cultures. They may not be flashy, but they have substance.

When I meet someone seeking investment who exudes ego, I predict they are headed for a crash. They may have many of the right qualities, but can they get out of their own way? I've developed the ability to determine very quickly whether someone is coming from a place of humility or hubris.

Here are behaviors that tip me off to hubris:

- They start every sentence with "I."
- They pound their chest about this or that.
- They are seldom wrong, never in doubt.
- They say (or imply), "I'm not insecure. I know exactly what I'm going to do." And then they fall off a cliff instead of insecurely making sure they validate the plan.
- They exude confidence rather than embracing insecurity about what they do not know.

- They act smug and need to be the smartest ones in the room. They seem to say, "Shut up and listen to me. I know what I'm talking about."
- People with hubris interrupt others.
- Their attitude is the opposite of this quip by Robert Newton Peck, "Never miss an opportunity…to keep your mouth shut."[1]

I want to hear what others have to say, and I also want to work with people who listen. We all start by not knowing. So, we admit we don't know. We should create a culture that ejects people who pound their chests.

A few years ago, a colleague introduced me to a CEO with such an ego that he would interrupt you every time you started to say something. I watched this behavior in a strategic planning meeting, as he repeatedly interrupted everyone to tell them why they were wrong. He probably *was* the smartest one in the room because his toxic insecurity had prevented him from hiring anyone more talented.

At that point, I pulled the plug on our relationship. I felt sorry for him because he had been building his company for several years, and I knew he would never get anywhere until he could get his hubris under control. He was self-funding his business, but I felt he would not get ahead until he could get out of his own way.

I don't do this often but wanted to get his attention. I told him as kindly as I could, "You need to address a prob-

1 Robert Newton Peck, first appeared in *A Day No Pigs Would Die, (Oregon City: Laurel-Leaf Books, 1994).*

lem, which is that you think you're smarter than everyone else. That may or may not be true, but you won't accomplish anything by making that the modus operandi for your business." He was not CEO material. Not yet anyway.

Conversely, I met a dermatologist about a new venture recently. Surgeons and doctors are stereotyped as being egomaniacs, but this man maintained his humility. He was a delight. I knew our relationship would only get better. He was what we were looking for on our team.

I believe everyone has "the right stuff" to succeed. Everyone can learn to listen, scan the data, and question their assumptions. I'd be wasting my time on this book if I believed these traits were only inborn.

FLAMING ASSHOLES

There is a common misconception that success requires a big ego. This misconception has worsened as reality TV and social media have turned the real world into a funhouse-mirror version of itself. I coached a talented entrepreneur a while back who relayed this to me. I will paraphrase:

> My partner and I noticed that people who are mega-successful seem to be flaming assholes. He and I talked about it and wondered: do we even want success at that level if that's what it takes? Maybe we don't. That's not who we are. Then we met Jim, and he's so kind. It has been a revelation that you don't have to be like that.

That's such an important takeaway: *You don't have to be an asshole.* While I have met a few assholes in business, the people who have had the greatest success for the longest time embodied humility.

The best leaders have genuine humility, whereas flaming assholes tend to flame out. Their toxic insecurity gets the best of them in the end. French novelist Honoré de Balzac wrote, "Nothing is a greater impediment to being on good terms with others than being ill at ease with yourself."[2]

DON'T CONFUSE YOUR WORK WITH YOUR IDENTITY

Here is a sneaky ego trap that I want to get on your radar because it's one that even those with altruistic motives can fall into. When people passionately commit to their work and do it to benefit others, they can start believing that they *are* their work. You are not your job, your title, or your business. You're not your art or any other creative endeavor.

Your purpose in life is much bigger than any of that.

What would happen to your sense of identity if you lost your job tomorrow? What if your company fails? You might be heartbroken, but would you be shattered?

I am reminded of how a doctor expressed his purpose in a near-death experience book I read recently called *Quarks of Light*. In it, the author, Rob A. Gentile, asked one of the people who helped save his life, "When did you realize that your purpose was to become a doctor? You seem so well suited

2 Honoré de Balzac, https://www.brainyquote.com/authors/honore-de-balzac-quotes

for this. I can't imagine you being anything else." His doctor corrected him, "My *vocation* is being a doctor," he said. "My *purpose* is to know God."[3]

I believe our purpose is to know God and to serve others. That is why we should do work of value as a gift for others. Once you give a gift, it is no longer yours. You don't control how people receive it or what happens when forces beyond you grasp hold of it. Create as a servant of the work and then release it to the world without expectation. Even if you have a calling, you serve the work. You are not the work, no matter how important it is.

RECOGNIZE IF YOU NEED COACHING OR THERAPY

Do you want to change? If you've read this far, I trust that you do.

Do you believe you can? I do.

Practicing the discipline of humility requires deliberate effort. Are you willing to do the work? How committed are you to practicing the habits discussed in this book? Have you begun rehearsing the phrases below?

- "Tell me more."
- "What am I missing?"
- "I'm listening."

If not, why haven't you? Is it that you don't believe me, or are you procrastinating?

---

3 Rob A. Gentile, *Quarks of Light: A Near Death Experience, (Fresno: Ignite Press, 2021), 157.*

Angela Duckworth recommends therapy to work on deep-seated issues. It isn't always easy to change ways of looking at life that have been with us since childhood. She also notes that cognitive behavioral therapy (CBT) has an even more lasting impact than anti-depression medication. Therapeutic journaling is another tool.

JOURNALING

I begin most days by journaling. You may also benefit from an honest journaling practice for evaluating your behaviors and working to change your mindsets. A journal like this is not the kind you leave for posterity but a private one only for you.

Journaling can get swirling thoughts out of your head so you have space for creative work. No good comes from letting thorny issues repeat in your mind. Get it out of there and into the light so you can deal with it. Once on the page, clarity often emerges, and fears have a way of becoming manageable. An empowering exercise to try is naming your fears one by one. By drawing them out and giving them a name, unhealthy emotions are exposed to the disinfecting power of sunlight. This act drains them of their power and returns it to you.[4]

Processing your frustrations will help you proceed more deliberately. A journal can be a place to dump animosity, get your heart in the right place, and thoughtfully work out conversations you may need to have.

---

4 Brené Brown, *Atlas of the Heart*, (New York: Random House, 2021, Kindle edition), xxv.

Countless famous authors have said variations on this quote: "I write to figure out what I think." Journaling is a low-pressure way to process your bouts with toxic insecurity and hubris.

My co-author is a proponent of Julia Cameron-style morning pages for this purpose. It is a prescriptive process pioneered in the bestselling book *The Artist's Way.*[5] The basic idea is to write precisely three full pages of longhand, stream-of-consciousness musings in a notebook as soon as you wake up.

Some people advocate throwing them away, which increases authenticity and frees you from fears of judgment. What you write is totally up to you, although this is a great place for both gratitude and naming your fears. Cameron is, however, prescriptive about how the method works. Keep your pen moving and do it every day whether you feel like it or not. The length matters: stop once you've covered three pages.

In addition, therapeutic journaling is another evidence-based treatment for working through trauma and other issues.[6] The United States Department of Veteran Affairs reports that therapeutic journaling has been shown to be as effective as therapy.

> Over the past 25 years, a growing body of research has demonstrated the beneficial effects that writing about traumatic or stressful events has on

---

5 Julia Cameron, *The Artist's Way: A Spiritual Path to Higher Creativity, 25th Anniversary Edition*, (New York: Tarcher, 2016), 9.

6 Rhonda Lauritzen, "How to Start or Boost a Journal Writing Habit," https://evalogue.life/journal-writing/

> physical and emotional health. Therapeutic journaling is associated with both short-term improvements and long-term decreases in health problems such as immune system functioning. People who are going through health problems, breakups, grief, natural disasters, and unemployment have all been shown to have significant and substantial short-term reductions in post-traumatic stress and depressive symptoms.[7]

THERAPY OR COACHING

If you exhibit behaviors that come from entrenched feelings of fear and defensiveness, or if you find yourself displaying habits of toxic insecurity, you may need to do some deeper work. You need to plug the hole in your bucket because no amount of accolades will ever fill it. Learn to embrace self-love and cultivate confident humility, so you don't take out your deficiencies on others.

If you're committed to success, then you will do the work. Everyone who performs at elite athletic levels has a coach. Are you better than a professional sports player? Do the work. Start now.

7 Shilagh A. Mergain and Janice Singles, "Therapeutic Journaling," US Department of Veterans Affairs: Whole Health Library, 2016 (updated 2023), https://www.va.gov/WHOLEHEALTHLIBRARY/tools/therapeutic-journaling.asp#:~:text=Therapeutic%20journaling%20is%20the%20process%20of%20writing%20down,and%20problems%20that%20we%20may%20be%20struggling%20with.

Remember that cognitive behavioral therapy focuses on helping you change your behaviors and is more effective than medication in the long run.

Investing in yourself is one of the most profitable decisions you could ever make. You are your most valuable asset. Treat yourself as such.

SECTION THREE

ASSEMBLING A COMPANY

CHAPTER 13

Hire People Better Than You Who Want Your Job

I read that Clint Eastwood is still making movies in his nineties and loving it. Is that being a workaholic? No, it's passion. When the late Toby Keith asked Eastwood how he does it, he replied, "I just get up every morning and go out. And I don't let the old man in." Keith thought that line would make a good hook for a song, and then he wrote one for an Eastwood movie, *The Mule*.[1]

My colleague Larry Watts added his perspective about working together:

> You need the sense that your values are personally aligned with the company and to think of it as the highest and best use of your time. You only have one life, and then you die. Find someplace where your talents, values, and ambitions are in sync with

1 Cathy Applefeld Olson, "Toby Keith Explains How Clint Eastwood Inspired 'Don't Let the old Man In' for 'The Mule'", *Billboard, 12/15/2018,)* https://www.billboard.com/music/music-news/toby-keith-clint-eastwood-inspired-dont-let-the-old-man-in-the-mule-interview-8490429/) accessed June 20, 2024

> the rest of the organization. If that's not where you are, leave it and start or join another one. And if you keep doing outstanding work and others see you as someone who always helps, you won't have trouble finding another job. It will find you.

My goal is to get people more excited on Monday morning than Friday night because they've developed a passion for what we're doing, which fuels everything else. I pity people who spend five days hating their job and live for weekends so they can do whatever they enjoy. "Hump day" and "TGIF" have to do with hating to be at work. On Wednesday, your week is half over, and on Friday: "Thank God it's over, so we can go out and party." That's sad to me. I've been blessed with coworkers who go back forty and fifty years, and they have been a source of immense joy in my life. I just got an email last week from someone who said, "If you start another company, I want to be a part of it because I've never had that feeling of excitement and passion since, and I want it again."

I want to create a joyful environment for others to join. When you're passionate, it's no longer work. My goal is to find people who already have the spark and empower them so they feel the same passion for their work that others might put into a hobby. It's a treat to do work you love with people you enjoy.

The worst word society has created is "workaholic" because it implies people are addicted to their work in a way that is unhealthy. Some people may drown themselves in long hours because they're numbing their feelings, but working with purpose is not that.

The journey of work is joyful, and it is more important than the arrival. The arrival is frequently like, "Okay, I got where I wanted to go. Now, what am I going to do?" If you have the passion, you will love the journey and the next one after. There are a few ways to build this kind of culture, and I want to share three that have worked for me.

HIRE PEOPLE WHO ARE THE BEST AT WHAT THEY DO

The first way to create a great culture is to hire people who are better than you and who want your job. That's easy to say, but people have a hard time doing it. They are afraid and feel threatened. Negative insecurity gets in their way.

If I'm the smartest person in the room, I'm in the wrong room.[2] I want to surround myself with people who are smarter than I am, which will make my job so much easier. This is all about humility. This isn't a competition; it's leveraging everyone's unique intelligence. I want people who are not only good—not only great—but who are the *best* at what they do. When you hire people like this, it would take extreme hubris to micromanage them because they have superior skills in their domain. Hiring the best people makes obvious the need to funnel authority to them. You don't want to waste their talent, so you empower them to move fast.

If you struggle with this, it's important to reframe your mindset to realize that people who are better than you will be extraordinarily knowledgeable. They will perform well, and this will only make you look better.

---

2 Unknown speaker, often attributed to Confucius and others.

At each of my companies, we hired a whole generation of self-starters who didn't need or want to be told what to do. They came to work with us because they wanted to change the world. For example, at Caremark, Roger Klotz was our National Director over Pharmacy Development. He is a gifted man who would live and die for patient care. He had been the head of clinical pharmacy at Children's Memorial Hospital in Chicago, where he used to do exotic dosing for the kids because the adult doses never worked. He often made rounds with nurses in patient rooms. He was exceptional and brought the highest level of integrity to our work,

Another person who brought wisdom and credibility to Caremark was the ultra-credentialed Dick Allen. He was a Yale undergrad, a Stanford MBA, and people loved him. I've mentioned Teri Louden before from CardioNet. I trusted her to launch a whole operation in Philadelphia. Larry Watts came with me through eight startups. Sue MacKinnon Zieg was one of the original five employees at Caremark and has been a colleague now for decades. When we hired her, she was just starting her career and learned with us on the job.

I could go on and on, and I worry about leaving so many others out. There were countless people who iterated the problems of product development and service delivery. Each one was essential.

Empower capable people like these to take risks. They will be willing to do so when you create an environment that does not punish failure. We've spent much of this book on the benefits of embracing failure during the iteration phase. For this to happen, you must build trust that makes people feel safe experimenting.

Give people clear authority and the boundaries around that authority. Then get out of the way. Likewise, ensure they are majoring in the majors and not bringing you all their minutiae. If you fall into that trap, you will be a bottleneck, and everything will grind to a halt.

The idea is to push decision-making down and delegate, delegate, delegate. Consider this math when you worry that others cannot perform as well as you: if they do 90 percent of the job you do, and you multiply that effort by ten people, that ten times ninety is a lot more than one times one hundred. I knew enough to know the kind of people I needed to hire who would guide the direction. The specialists knew far more in their areas of expertise than I ever could.

EMPOWER PEOPLE TO WRITE THEIR OWN JOB DESCRIPTIONS

When you bring in key talent, don't hem them in with a typical corporate job description. Instead, let them write their own. When I bring someone into the team, I approach them from the "you-point-of-view." I tell them, "I'm not going to give you a job description that you must shoehorn yourself into. We will start with a blank piece of paper and create a job description that will perfectly fit you because you wrote it."

That is such a freeing opportunity that people go wild with delight. They've never heard of such a thing before. People will give you their best work when it naturally aligns with their interests and passion. As the company grows, there will be pressure to standardize job descriptions, but I insist they be written in pencil because they will change quickly.

Before you hire, create a job announcement written from the "you-point-of-view" that conveys excitement about how a candidate will make a difference. I recently helped a founder hire a marketing director, and we wrote that type of job posting about the meaningful work this person would do. The idea was to get the candidate's blood pumping. We wanted them to think, *This job is exactly what I have prepared myself for*. We posted it and received thirty resumes in two hours, and they were of the highest caliber. For fun, here is that job announcement so you can see what I mean:

> You are a game changer. You ask how you can do something instead of focusing on why you can't. You are an out-of-the-box thinker who believes your organization needs to move faster than the current rate of change, not slower. You're impatient with your current organization. They are paralyzed by politics and are missing opportunities you know you could achieve. You are a contrarian who believes in coloring outside the lines when appropriate. You possess experience and talent and have demonstrated success to shred the accomplishments below. They are all familiar to you. You've accomplished them in the past. Your attitude is, "give me the authority and responsibility to accomplish our mutually defined goals and then get out of the way." Your role will be key in establishing the game-changing global future of this company so we can emerge as the market-defined leader. You'll make mistakes along the way.

> Learn from them and course-correct for greater success. If you possess these traits, desires, and accomplishments, make it happen.

Once you have a slate of candidates, ensure your interviewing process will gauge whether this person's values align and whether they have the wherewithal to do the job. Don't focus on how many years of experience they have or their grades, or you will chase away the best candidates.

Notice where people's talents naturally gravitate in the organization and adjust accordingly. Too often, people get in trouble for wanting to be part of something that isn't their job. When you see it happening naturally, change the job description, not the person. Eric Ries echoes this sentiment. "Some people are natural inventors who prefer to work without the pressure and expectations of the later business phases. Others are ambitious and see innovation as a path toward senior management.... People should be allowed to find the kinds of jobs that suit them best. In fact, entrepreneurship should be considered a viable career path for innovators inside large organizations."[3] This role in big companies has been dubbed, "intrapreneur."

Remember how we discussed that passion makes someone indefatigable? These ideas don't just apply to you. By adopting the ideas in this chapter, you can empower everyone in your organization to be in that same state.

When we became the leading provider for AIDS patients, we had experts warn us that we'd lose employees because they wouldn't want to go into homes and be exposed to the risks.

---

3 Ries, *The Lean Startup*, Audible audio edition.

We had zero problems with employees over this issue. Zero. That's because they were on a mission. They knew the patients as people and not just a diagnosis. They were proud of the company and what we stood for.

In the companies I founded, it was a competitive advantage that our employees were only one degree of separation from patients. We hired people who went into healthcare because they wanted to help people, and they were able to do that. At CardioNet, the people in the monitoring center talked to patients daily. These patients were frightened and hoping against hope that we could finally solve a life-threatening problem so they wouldn't die. And we did find solutions to those problems.

WHEN THE COMPANY IS GROWING FASTER THAN THE PEOPLE IN IT

When I founded my first company, I hired a guy who had a Stanford MBA—a very, very bright person. The company started growing like a weed, and he came into my office one day and said, "We've got to stop growing."

I said, "What do you mean we have to stop growing? Why?"

"Well, because I can't keep up with the reimbursement."

I looked at him and said, "Okay, hire more people."

I was incredulous, but he was also right. In business circles, there is what has been called "Packard's Law" from Hewlett-Packard. It states: "No company can grow revenues consistently faster than its ability to get enough of the right people to implement that growth and still become a great company."

That law is why it's so important to hire with the "you-point-of-view" and to empower people through their job descriptions. You will need great people, and you will need them fast. It is an intoxicating environment when a company is taking off like a rocket. There are opportunities everywhere, and it is gratifying.

There may come a time when your company is growing faster than everyone in it. You can hire a VP of marketing for a five-million-dollar company. Then, six months later, the company has doubled its growth, and you need a different skill set. The person you had before couldn't keep up with the change. This kind of growth requires frequent reorganization, and some people won't make the cut. If you hold up a mirror and show that VP the changes that have happened and what is needed from them now, they will usually take the initiative and move on voluntarily. Others might do well with a lateral move, but sadly, this is the exception.

I mentioned earlier that I know it's time for me to exit when politics set in. Another indication is when the task at hand throughout the company shifts from figuring out how to do what hasn't been done before to doing the same thing over and over. The company will need systems-builders and people who thrive in a stable environment. These are people who can help with modest, incremental gains.

The people early on who were "we're going to change the world" types will not necessarily share the same values as the ones who come in later when the company is already a success. That's just the nature of the cycle.

IT'S ALL ABOUT RESPECTING YOUR PEOPLE

Once again, having a dynamic company with amazing people comes down to respect. Your company's success is dependent on you respecting your team's talent, their areas of expertise, and their potential.

In life, your success and happiness are also dependent on respecting others. When I go out to eat, I ask the server's name and engage them in conversation because I care about them. I open the car door for my housekeeper. Everyone who serves you deserves the same respect as the president of the United States. Be sure you convey that attitude in all you do. It is believing in people. It is appreciating their differences, especially by realizing where their strengths may fill in for your weaknesses.

I am a contrarian. Larry Watts calls himself a dam builder. These are different personalities, but we complemented each other's strengths and weaknesses. Another weakness in my background is that I do not have an impressive formal education, and we were in an industry where credentials mattered. So, we hired some fantastic people with the background and credibility we needed. I've also hired brilliant women when the industry was primarily dominated by men. This hiring practice was a competitive advantage because we could attract first-rate talent that others overlooked. In one company, 100 percent of our salesforce consisted of women, most of whom were single mothers. They were some of the most productive workers we had because they wanted to get their job done and get home to their kids.

In our Philadelphia office for CardioNet, we employed a diverse and dedicated cast of front-line technicians. My point is that it was always a mosaic of talent, and I appreciated other people's strengths.

Building a culture of respect takes care of so much else. What does that look like? Respect shows in many ways, but I will give one example. For years, I have disseminated the following memo of expected meeting etiquette:

MEETING ETIQUETTE

The following is about mutual respect:

- Meetings start on time with you in attendance from the very beginning.
- You're never late for a meeting.
- Meetings end on time.
- Anyone who is invited to the meeting needs to be in the meeting.
- If anyone leaves, the meeting stops until they return.
- No sidebar conversations. Anything you are saying is important enough for everyone to hear.
- Anyone can declare a bio break at any time.
- No texting or reading emails during the meeting.
- Phones are muted during the meeting.

Ground rules like these have been instrumental in helping people be more excited on Monday morning than they are on Friday night. Too many organizations tolerate meetings that waste time and convey a lack of respect. That is terribly demotivating. It is imperative to create an environment that brings out the best in people and values their time. Great people want to be part of a team where this is the culture, and they have little patience for anything less.

CAMELOT

I hope you are blessed to work in a fast-growing environment where the mission matters and you are surrounded by talented, ethical people. Former colleagues have described this scenario as "Camelot." If you are the leader of something special, do all you can to preserve it. If you are part of the team, take advantage of all the opportunities. Don't get comfortable. Choose to grow along with the company because you are adaptable. Embracing insecurity will serve you well through the changes ahead.

There is no guarantee, however, that the way the company looks in the future will continue to be a good fit for you. As the company evolves, you may not appreciate the new culture. You might not enjoy your new duties. It might get sold to new owners who take it in a different direction.

At each juncture, look for serendipity. Look for circumstances to bring you what you need, even if it isn't what you want at the time. What can you learn from this new phase? What else might you do that will challenge you in new ways? What new opportunities might come your way? I believe that if you are open and willing to serve, your next assignment will arrive right on time.

CHAPTER 14

Get the First Breath Right

I was born a preemie and spent my first weeks in an incu bator. This had lifelong effects on my health. That is one reason I am so attuned to the phrase, "Get the first breath right." Think of when a baby is born. The first gulp of air is more important than those that follow. You must have that first gulp. That's the inspiration for your venture. That is the moment you know it's time to go for it. The first breath is the positive energy you have with your founding team. The first breath of your venture will set a tone. Will it be one of creative insecurity, or toxic insecurity? The first breath should start with a commitment to iterate rather than making everything perfect from the start. When you start with a culture of humility, the rest is a pleasure. In the early phases, you can set an example for others on your team of never giving up on your dreams by the way you navigate the inevitable obstacles.

Pay attention to how any new adventure begins. Beginnings matter. Things that start well typically only get better. But things that don't start well rarely get better.

Peter Thiel echoed my thoughts on this with what his colleagues dubbed "Thiel's law," which is that "A startup messed up at its foundation cannot be fixed."[1]

The first thing you do in life is inhale. Make that first breath a good one.

When a venture accelerates from the start, it bodes well for how things will go afterward. The opposite can indicate a hard road ahead. I see people investing too much time into an idea that can't catch momentum. I'm not saying startups are easy, but you should feel a sense of motion. You should see promising signs and feel energized. If you struggle to gain traction, you'd better examine why that is. Remember what we discussed in Chapter 10: don't marry a mistake. Know when to exit, whether that's an idea, a business, or a relationship. You are in trouble if your new venture begins with partner contention, a corrupt philosophy, or if the fundamentals aren't right.

I apply this lens to relationships of various types. If I'm considering an investment but see the red flags of hubris in a founder, I'll bow out. Contracts are also a litmus test for me. If a prospective partner sends me a reasonable contract, I will sign it with very few changes. If it's one-sided, I don't attempt to negotiate; I exit the relationship entirely because that contract reveals their philosophy. I know to expect more of the same from them in the future. This applies to other negotiations too. I want a win-win price, not by haggling where I start way at one end in my favor, and the other party comes

1 Thiel, *Zero to One*, 107.

from the opposite extreme. I will propose a reasonable price, and I do not like to dicker—I'm more likely to just walk away. I am not applying pressure as a negotiating tactic. Once I'm gone, I don't look back.

Likewise, when seeking investors, don't mess up a good thing by being obsessed with dilution and control. Nine times out of ten, entrepreneurs are freakish about maintaining control. The way to create value that grows from millions to billions is by *letting go* of control. Value creation is about spreading the wealth, not keeping it to yourself. If you find compatible investors, create a strong plan for spending their money. I love dilution and want more of it—as long as it increases my overall value. I am a lot less worried about dilution and more concerned about the size of pie we are splitting. You want a mathematical calculation that makes you wealthier. If you are obsessed with calling all the shots, you will also repel good partners and employees, and you will push opportunities away. If you try to contain your work in your own two hands, you risk strangling it. Get the first breath right by opening the clutches of your fists. Share ownership and power with good people and according to a good plan. I find that tendencies toward being a control freak stem from toxic insecurity.

Another way to get the first breath right is to conduct a premortem like we discussed in Chapter 5. Voicing and addressing concerns also preempts passive-aggressive team members from naysaying in unhelpful ways later. Instead, you can show strong leadership by communicating to your team: "If you have something to say, say it now. We will address it and tackle the challenges together. We'll maintain a healthy respect for the dangers, mitigating them rather than pretending they don't exist. If we uncover a fatal flaw, we'll go in another direction."

Setting that tone helps gets the first breath right.

YOU DON'T HAVE TO BE THE CEO

If you have ever felt like a misfit in bureaucracy, you must have wondered how to get out of that constraining environment. Preparing to start your own contrarian business might be the right move, or you might do better joining a team. You've probably heard conflicting advice ranging from "You should start your own business" to "Don't quit your day job."

As I have said throughout this book, it makes sense for most people to gain experience in an industry before starting their own company. Most people have some growing up to do before they're ready. It can also take time to build some runway and establish credibility so others will come aboard. There are long odds against any venture succeeding, but the odds improve when you have prepared.

Also, consider where you are in your journey of embracing creative insecurity. Before you start your own business, honestly assess your strengths and weaknesses and then work on vision, the no-quit gene, and humility. Get comfortable leaning into insecurity.

You may be entrepreneurially minded but still crave a greater degree of security than a founder will have. If this is you, you may find a rewarding path by joining a more established company that is growing quickly. Join a high-growth organization whose work lights your fire. Doing so may be less risky if you don't have a founder's temperament. The best bet for many bright people is to throw their energy into a team that shows promise rather than starting their own companies. Employees of Caremark who we interviewed as part of this book described it as a golden time, like being part of Camelot. I am grateful for the talented people who made our success possible. Many of them did very well financially by being part of what we built.

There are different personalities, and I'm not suggesting everyone should be like me. I have too many flaws. Companies need people who are good at coloring inside the lines and working within many layers of the organization. You can still contribute greatly to the mission if you are an "inside the lines" person.

If you want to start something but don't yet know what that is, my advice is to bide your time and follow the guidance outlined in Angela Duckworth's *Grit* to discover your area of interest. The time to start a business is when you have identified a pressing customer need that aligns with your interest. You can't force it; you will know when you have found both.

When you're ready to start something new, review The Contrarian's Checklist in the Appendix to vet your big idea.

ASSESSING YOUR STRENGTHS AS A FOUNDER

A self-aware founder or CEO will recognize which growth phase of a company best suits their strengths. For example, some people shine when shepherding early-stage companies but should exit when it comes time to scale. Only some founders are CEO material, and only a select few are well-suited for the later stages of an organization's growth. Some founders can grow into the CEO role, but others are better off stepping aside for professional leadership to take the helm. Neither early-stage founders nor growth CEOs are more important than the other; they're just different.

Steve Jobs is an interesting contrast to my personality where I started many companies and he stuck with one. He loved his company fiercely and was dedicated to growing it through all the phases. He continually reinvented Apple and pushed it toward perfection. He was thrilled by the constant challenges that one company presented, never getting bored. He said his greatest invention was Apple, not a particular product. He did not seem to have a hint of wanderlust. In other words, Jobs was not a serial entrepreneur—he remained wedded to Apple for life.

You can and should grow your skills, but don't try to change your personality. There have been great lieutenants, founders, and CEOs of all stripes. Know thyself. Are you a cheetah or a dam builder? Do you love new beginnings or growing an existing idea?

Regardless of your strengths, the mindset of creative insecurity will benefit you, and you can learn it. The traits of the Contrarian's Trifecta will keep you in check whether you are a founder or a lieutenant.

As we close our time together in this book, I want to share the story of a young woman who first came into my life as a housekeeper. Lanae entered foster care at the age of five from an abusive family whose parents went to prison. They made her surname notorious among local law enforcement. She is a petite person who fought her way through youth as a scrapper, regularly getting into trouble for dustups. As a teen, she repeatedly ran away from her foster families, lashing out at those who tried to help her. When she aged out of foster care, she became a recreational cage fighter. It might not have been the healthiest outlet, but she was born with the no-quit gene in spades.

Although still early in her journey, Lanae has already lived several lifetimes, transforming into a lovely, sharp young woman. You would never guess her history from a casual conversation. She has been through some hell and is now committed to helping others. Today, she is working on her education so she can make a difference for kids in the foster care system. Lanae sees where change is needed in that system, and she believes it is possible. She is a contrarian.

I also see Lanae's remarkable ability to forgive and put herself in the shoes of people who gave her tough love. Although she experienced abuse and has seen some terrible things, Lanae is not bitter. She credits caring social workers for teaching her the skills to land on her feet, and she cautions other youth about returning to old environments plagued by drugs and violence. She has both gratitude and empathy.

I've been the recipient of Lanae's kindness too. She often shares with me quotes and inspirational videos she thinks will be relevant for me. Her habit reminds me of myself at her age, devouring books on positive thinking and repeating affirmations. Recently, I asked how she managed to claw her way out, and she said, "There has always been the voice of God in my head, telling me that I was meant for more." She has vision, and she is shooting for the stars.

She also thanked me for reinforcing her positive choices and for seeing her as someone worthy of my time. I thought, *How could I not?* Her potential is evident. She may have felt like a misfit in the past, but she has a brilliant future ahead. I have seen her talk with people thirty years her senior, and they lean in because she is not only insightful, but she also speaks from the heart.

Lanae exemplifies what I hope you believe about yourself—that you're destined for greater heights than what others may believe you can achieve.

If people have underestimated you, don't waste energy trying to prove them wrong. Double down—right now—on proving yourself right. Learn to love the ways you have felt like a misfit in the past, because the world needs your unique perspective. Stay humble, envision a bright future, and never give up on your dreams. Change the world by leaning into instead of away from your insecurities and journey into the unknown.

APPENDIX A

The Contrarian's Checklist

You can get a printable version of this at: https://creativein-security.com

DO YOU HAVE A BIG IDEA?

An essential part of entrepreneurship is vetting your big ideas. It's too easy to fall in love with your idea and fail to see a fatal flaw. As I am mentoring entrepreneurs in business and others in my work with the Stephen Ministry, I walk them through a series of Socratic questions to help them discover their own answers. My questions use branching logic, so there is no set formula, but as Rhonda and I worked on this book, we pulled from actual sessions with entrepreneurs and compiled a checklist to simulate the process.

Keep this checklist handy if you seek funding because it will help you prepare. You may download a printable version on our website at https://creativeinsecurity.com.

MAJOR IN THE MAJORS

- What is the magnitude of the problem you are trying to solve?
- What is the total market size if you captured 100 percent of it?
- Will this idea move the needle for customers? Can you quantify this?

It takes as much time to do a big idea as a small one. I often tell entrepreneurs, "This is an interesting idea, but you're not thinking big enough. Let's take this and make it into a much bigger company than you're looking at."

Stop focusing on minutiae and focus on big wins. Remember to major in the majors. Don't major in the minors.

Is it a billion-dollar idea? While money isn't important, the impact is, so we use money as a measuring stick. You can substitute another type of impact for the notion of a "billion-dollar idea" if you are involved in a nonprofit or humanitarian effort. The point is to go big. The best ideas solve critical problems for customers.

IS IT A PRODUCT, OR IS IT A BUSINESS?

- Is your idea a single product idea, or can it expand to become an entire business?
- Does the product involve repeat purchases? For how long in a customer's life? What are the related add-ons?
- What is the lifetime value of each customer compared to the acquisition cost?

You want to build a brand that customers will come back for again and again. It's difficult to sustain a one-off product, especially in a narrow niche and when the price is low.

IS YOUR SOLUTION HEAD-SLAPPINGLY OBVIOUS?

- Is your solution so compelling that when people hear it, they slap their foreheads and say, "Why didn't I think of that?"
- Is it simple enough that they immediately get it?

People may not understand the technology, but your target customer should grasp the problem and solution without complex explanations. Tell a memorable story to illustrate your concept. When I sit through a founder's presentation with slide after slide of detail, I get concerned they don't know how to major in the majors.

IS THIS IDEA DIFFERENT AND NEW?

- What is the competition? There should be no meaningful competition, or your new development should be ten times better than what anybody else is doing.
- You want a novel idea, as opposed to copying somebody else.

Don't be a commodity in a sea of commodities. Important ideas make a new contribution to the world, not minor improvements on known problems. Avoid competition by being a contrarian.

CAN YOU BE FIRST?

- Can you be the first to do it right?
- Are you paralyzed by indecision or fear?

Being first is more important than being right. You can be first only once; you can be right later. Everything will require modification, so move swiftly and boldly. Give yourself permission to "fail your way to success." You will figure out the right way if you are in motion.

WHO IS ON THE TEAM?

- Does your founding team have experience in the industry, along with maturity and humility?
- Do they understand the market and product?
- Do they listen and accept coaching, or do they need to be the smartest person in the room?

Create an environment that attracts the very best people, and where those people have the latitude to create their own job descriptions around their unique strengths. Bring in people who will enhance a culture of humility, not toxic insecurity. Everything that comes later will be easier when built on this foundation.

HOW COMMITTED ARE YOU?

- Does the team possess the "no-quit gene?"
- Is the team more excited on Monday morning than they are on Friday night?

Remember this adage: if at first you don't succeed, try a thousand times.

BUT ARE YOU MARRYING A MISTAKE?

- Have you encountered any insurmountable obstacles?
- What yellow flags do you see?

As you validate your idea, it is vital to hold your no-quit gene in check with an openness to understanding market factors and practical limits. Remember the natural tension between the "no-quit gene" and knowing when to quit. Hold this paradox in balance.

Be prepared to pivot and find another way, another market, or another idea if it doesn't validate. In other words, "don't marry a mistake." There are many ideas and approaches you will quit along the way. Run down any yellow flags to make sure they don't turn into red flags.

DO YOU HAVE THE NECESSARY RESOURCES?

- What will it take to develop the technology or create the prototype?
- How will you market it?
- When will you run out of cash?

Do you have enough runway to get liftoff? As you seek investment, don't obsess over control and dilution of ownership. If the fundamentals are sound, resources will follow.

Craft a strong plan for how you will spend the money to grow the company, and you'll come out ahead. Just make sure that dilution is on an up round, not a down round. Focus on increasing your overall value.

WHAT IS YOUR GO-TO MARKET STRATEGY?

- What will be your marketing and distribution strategy? Is there enough margin to cover your customer acquisition cost and overhead?
- What will your margins look like at scale?
- What can your ideal customer afford to pay?

Will you employ a push strategy through distribution partners or pull products through the pipeline with strong marketing? What will the costs and margins be at each layer in the supply chain?

WHAT IS YOUR BELL COW?

- What is the best, most prestigious target or client you could land?

The principle is that after you have validated your idea, pick the most influential customer and create success there. It's okay to work out some bugs on a less consequential account first, but don't stay at that level long. On a farm, the lead cow has a bell around its neck, and the rest follow the leader. Once you have been successful with a prestigious target, others will get in line.

WHAT IS YOUR ELEVATOR PITCH?

- When you practice delivering a thirty-second summary of your idea, do people immediately say, "Tell me more?"
- Does your pitch answer why this is different from anything they have ever seen?

You haven't nailed it if your listeners don't light up with curiosity. Break your idea into its simplest components, tell a compelling story, and polish your delivery until it sings.

WHAT ARE PEOPLE'S QUESTIONS ABOUT YOUR IDEA?

- As you practice your elevator pitch, what questions do people ask?
- Listen intently, write questions down, and prepare answers.
- Get comfortable being insecure about what you don't know by asking, "What am I missing?"

Practice and prepare answers based on reaction to the practice runs. Pro tip: show financial assumptions before projections. If the assumptions are not believable, you'll lose your audience.

HAVE YOU CONDUCTED A "PREMORTEM?"

- If you were to predict causes of death for your idea, what would they be?

Conduct an exercise whereby team members take turns predicting why your business may fail. The point is to not let people smugly say, "I told you so," if it does fail later. The point is to get ahead of it. Every business will have multiple "near-death experiences." By identifying possible causes of death, you can avoid them.

We hope you will use this checklist to review your opportunities, evaluate your risks, and double down on an idea that is worthy of your talents. Remember that it takes as much time to bring a big idea as a small one into the world, so make it count. You can use your energy to change the world and your life for the better.

REVIEW INQUIRY

Hey, it's Jim and Rhonda here. We hope you've enjoyed the book, finding it both inspirational and practical. We have a favor to ask you.

Would you consider giving it a rating wherever you bought the book? Stores are more likely to promote a book when they feel good about its content, and reader reviews are a grate barometer for a book's quality.

So please go to the website for wherever you bought the book, search for the book title, and leave a review. We even encourage you to include a picture of you holding the book, which increases the likelihood that your review will be accepted.

Many thanks in advance,
Jim Sweeney and Rhonda Lauritzen

BIBLIOGRAPHY

Beard, Allison. "Life's Work: An Interview with Tina Turner," *Harvard Business Review*, January–February 2021, https://hbr.org/2021/01/lifes-work-an-interview-with-tina-turner.

Berkman, Leslie. "Executive Comes Full Circle in Deal for Lab: Acquisitions: The Former marketing director of McGaw Laboratories heads a group that is acquiring his old employer, now known as Kendall McGaw Laboratories," *Los Angeles Times*, August 1, 1990, https://www.latimes.com/archives/la-xpm-1990-08-01-fi-1609-story.html.

Berlin, Isiah. *The Hedgehog And the Fox*, (UK: Weidenfeld & Nicholson, 1953).

Brown, Brené. *Atlas of the Heart*, (New York: Random House, 2021, Kindle edition).

Brown, Brené. *Braving the Wilderness: The Quest for True Belonging and the Courage to Stand Alone*, (New York: Random House, 2017, Kindle Edition).

Burton, Thomas. "Visionary's reward: Combine 'Simple Ideas' And Some Failures; Result: Sweet Revenge: James Sweeney Bought Back His Old Company Cheap; Never Give up, He says," *Wall Street Journal*, February 3, 1995: A1. Accessed via *Wall Street Journal* Archives, New York Public Library.

Cameron, Julia. *The Artist's Way: A Spiritual Path to Higher Creativity, 25th Anniversary Edition*, (New York: Tarcher, 2016).

Carreyrou, John. "Hot Startup Theranos Has Struggled With Its Blood-Test Technology," Wall Street Journal, October 15, 2015, https://www.wsj.com/articles/theranos-has-struggled-with-blood-tests-1444881901, accessed June 20, 2024.

Carreyrou, John. *Bad Blood* (New York: Knopf, 2018), p. 224

Carroll, Lewis. Lewis Carroll, *Alice in Wonderland.* Quote accessed from Goodreads https://www.goodreads.com/quotes/642816-if-you-don-t-know-where-you-are-going-any-road, June 17, 2024.

Christensen, Clayton M. *The innovator's dilemma: The revolutionary book that will change the way you do business.* New York: Harper Business, 2011.

Churchill, Winston. "Never give in, never, never, never." Speech, Harrow School, October 29, 1941, Accessed from https://www.nationalchurchillmuseum.org/never-give-in-never-never-never.html, June 17, 2024.

Claxton, Guy. "Investigating human intuition: Knowing without knowing why," British Psychological Society, May 18, 1988.

Clear, James. *Atomic Habits*, (New York: Avery, 2018).

Collins, Jim, and Morten T. Hansen. *Great by Choice: Uncertainty, Chaos, and Luck—Why Some Thrive Despite Them All*, (New York: HarperCollins, 2011), Kindle Edition.

Collins, Jim. *Good to Great*, (New York: Harper Business, 2001, Kindle Edition).

Collins, Jim. "How Do You Do 'Stop Doing,'" (jimcollins.com, 2017), transcript of audio, https://www.jimcollins.com/media_topics/StopDoing.html.

Collins, Jim. *Good to Great: Why Some Companies Make the Leap & Others Don't*, (HarperCollins. Kindle Edition).

Collins, Jim. *How the Mighty Fall*, (JimCollins.com, 2009 Audible audiobook edition), 4 hrs., 41 min.

Cosgrove, Toby. *The Cleveland Clinic Way*, (New York: McGraw Hill Education, 2014).

Cosgrove, Toby, (Personal interview with the authors, January 24, 2024).

Covey, Steven. *The 7 Habits of Highly Effective People, "Habit 2: Begin With the End in Mind* https://www.franklincovey.com/the-7-habits/habit-2/. Franklin Covey. Accessed June 7, 2024.

Cuddy, Amy. "Your Body Language May Shape Who You Are," TED Talks, June 2012, TED.com, video, 20:45. https://www.ted.com/talks/amy_cuddy_your_body_language_may_shape_who_you_are.

Drucker, Peter. *The Effective Executive*, (New York: Harper & Row, hardcover edition).

Duckworth, Angela. *Grit: The Power of Passion and Perseverance*, (New York: Scribner, 2016), Kindle Edition.

Gentile, Rob A. *Quarks of Light: A Near Death Experience*, (Fresno: Ignite Press, 2021).

Gilbert, Elizabeth. *Big Magic: Creative Living Beyond Fear*, (Penguin Audio, 2015), Audible audiobook edition, 5 hrs., 5 min.

Gladwell, Malcolm. "Hallelujah," 7/28/2016, in *Revisionist History*, produced by Pushkin, podcast, 44:12 (excerpt begins at 25:33), https://www.pushkin.fm/podcasts/revisionist-history/hallelujah.

Gladwell, Malcom. "Complexity and the Ten-Thousand-Hour Rule," (*The New Yorker*) https://www.newyorker.com/sports/sporting-scene/complexity-and-the-ten-thousand-hour-rule, accessed June 20, 2024

Gladwell, Malcom, *Outliers*, (Hachette Audio, Audible audiobook version, 2008) 7 hr., 18 min.

Gladwell, Malcolm. "The Sure Thing," *The New Yorker*, January 10, 2010, https://www.newyorker.com/magazine/2010/01/18/the-sure-thing.

Gladwell, Malcolm. *Blink: The Power of Thinking Without Thinking*, (New York: Little, Brown and Company, 2005, Kindle Edition).

Godin, Seth. *Seth's Blog, The Certain Shortcut*, https://seths.blog/2013/05/the-certain-shortcut/.

Godin, Seth. *The Dip: A Little Book that Teaches You When to Quit (and When to Stick)*, (Audible Studios, 2007), Audible Audiobook edition. 1 hr., 32 min.

Grant, Adam. *Originals*, (New York: Penguin Publishing Group. Kindle Edition, 2016)

Grant, Adam. *Think Again:* (New York: Penguin Books, 2017), Kindle Edition.

Grant, Adam. *Think Again: The Power of Knowing What You Don't Know*, (New York: Penguin Books, 2023).

Grenny, Joseph, Kerry Patterson, Ron McMillan, Al Switzer, and Emily Gregory, *Crucial Conversations: Tools for Talking When Stakes Are High*, (New York: McGraw Hill, 2002).

Harrell, Eben. "Life's Work: An Interview with Alex Honnold," *Harvard Business Review*, May–June 2021, https://hbr.org/2021/05/lifes-work-an-interview-with-alex-honnold.

Hawk, Tiffany. *Breakthrough Book Proposal* online course, March 2023.

Hawk, Tiffany, "Writers and Rejection: Why You Don't Need A Thicker Skin." https://www.tiffanyhawk.com/blog/why-you-dont-need-a-thicker-skin, accessed June 24, 2024.

Hopkins, Anthony. Quotes. BrainyQuote.com, BrainyMedia Inc, 2024, https://www.brainyquote.com/quotes/anthony_hopkins_737840, accessed May 15, 2024.

Iskowitz, Marc. "What the Elizabeth Holmes verdict could mean for marketing." (*Medical Marketing and Media, January 7, 2022* https://www.mmm-online.com/home/channel/7-day-supply/what-the-elizabeth-holmes-verdict-could-mean-for-marketing/), Accessed June 20, 2024

Keller, Gary, and Jay Papasan. *The ONE Thing: The Surprisingly Simple Truth About Extraordinary Results*, Rellek Publishing Partners, Ltd, 2013), Audible Audiobook edition, 5 hr. 28 min.

King, Stephen. *On Writing: A Memoir of the Craft*, (New York: Pocket Books, 2000), 29.

Klein, Gary. *Performing a Premortem*, (Harvard Business Review), September 2007.

Krostof, Nicholas. "How Can You Hate Me When You Don't Even Know Me?" op-ed, *New York Times*, June 26, 2021, https://www.nytimes.com/2021/06/26/opinion/racism-politics-daryl-davis.html.

L'Engle, Madelaine. *A Circle of Quiet*, (New York: Farrar, Straus, and Giroux, 1972).

Lauritzen, Rhonda. *Richard Paul Evans Quotes from Author Training*, https://evalogue.life/Richard-paul-evans-quotes/ accessed June 16, 2024.

Lauritzen, Rhonda. "How to Start or Boost a Journal Writing Habit," https://evalogue.life/journal-writing/, accessed June 16, 2024.

Learning.com, *Defining Computational Thinking*, 2022. https://www.learning.com/blog/defining-computational-thinking/, Accessed June 12, 2024.

Leggett, Hadley. "Oct. 30, 1958: Medical Oops Leads to First Coronary Angiogram," *WIRED*, October 30, 2009, https://www.wired.com/2009/10/1030first-coronary-angiogram/.

Long, Bill. Personal interview with authors, October 6, 2022

McGrath, Rita. "Failing by Design," *Harvard Business Review*, April 2011, https://hbr.org/2011/04/failing-by-design.

Meissner, Hans-Otto. *Magda Goebbels: The First Lady of the Third Reich.* (New York: The Dial Press, 1978, rev. 1980).

Mergain Shilagh A, and Janice Singles. "Therapeutic Journaling," US Department of Veterans Affairs: Whole Health Library, 2016 (updated 2023). https://www.va.gov/WHOLEHEALTHLIBRARY/tools/therapeutic-journaling.asp#:~:text=Therapeutic%20journaling%20is%20the%20process%20of%20writing%20down,and%20problems%20that%20we%20may%20be%20struggling%20with.

Moorhouse, Roger. *Berlin at War* (New York: Basic Books, Kindle Edition 2010), 51.

National Social Anxiety Center. "Public Speaking Anxiety," accessed May 15, 2024, https://nationalsocialanxietycenter.com/social-anxiety/public-speaking-anxiety/.

Nien-hê, Hsieh, Christina R. Wing, Emilie Fournier, and Anna Resman. "Theranos: Who Has Blood on Their Hands? (A)." Harvard Business School Case 619-039, February 2019. (Revised February 2020.) https://www.hbs.edu/faculty/Pages/item.aspx?num=55760.

Olson, Cathy Applefeld, "Toby Keith Explains How Clint Eastwood Inspired 'Don't Let the old Man In' for 'The Mule'", *Billboard*, 12/15/2018,) https://www.billboard.com/music/music-news/toby-keith-clint-eastwood-inspired-dont-let-the-old-man-in-the-mule-interview-8490429/) accessed June 20, 2024.

Pearson, Joel. *The Intuition Toolkit: The New Science of Knowing What Without Knowing Why.*

Peck, Robert Newton. First appeared in *A Day No Pigs Would Die*, (Oregon City: Laurel-Leaf Books, 1994).

Peterson Kathy. Personal interview with Rhonda Lauritzen, October 5, 2018. See also Evalogue.Life, "The Untold History of the Ephraim Relief Society Granary," YouTube, video, 3:50, https://www.youtube.com/watch?v=Y7L1Qtjskdc&t=3s.

Pressfield, Steven. *The Artist's Journey*, (New York: Black Irish Entertainment LLC, 2018).

Ries, Eric. *The Lean Startup: How Today's Entrepreneurs Use Continuous Innovation to Create Radically Successful Businesses*, Read by the author, (New York: Random House, 2011), Audible audio edition, 8 hr., 38 min.

Robinson, Sir Ken. "Do Schools Kill Creativity?" TED Talks, February 2006, YouTube, video, 20:03, https://www.youtube.com/watch?v=iG9CE55wbtY.

Rubin, Rick. *The Creative Act: A Way of Being*, (New York: Penguin, 2023).

Ryan, Cornelius. *The Last Battle*, (New York: Pocket Books, 1967).

Schleckser, Jim. "Nelson Mandela's Secret to Winning," *Inc. Magazine*, June 21, 2016, https://www.inc.com/jim-schleckser/nelson-mandela-s-secret-to-winning.html.

Shane, Scott *The Illusions of Entrepreneurship*, (Yale University Press, 2008).

Sitkin, S.B. "Learning Through Failure: The Strategy of Small Losses." *Research in Organizational Behavior* 14, (January 1, 1992).

Smith, Rick. *The Leap: How 3 simple changes can propel your career from good to great*. New York: Portfolio, 2014.

Solov, Diane. "From C's and D's to Clinic's helm, Delos 'Toby' Cosgrove, surgeon, inventor, go-to guy (and dyslexic), finds the job opportunity he's been looking for." *The Plain Dealer*, last updated June 4, 2014, https://www.cleveland.com/pdextra/2014/06/from_cs_and_ds_to_clinics_helm.html.

The Wall Street Journal. "Visionary's reward: Combine 'Simple Ideas' and Some Failures; Result: Sweet Revenge: James Sweeney Bought Back His Old Company Cheap; Never Give up, He says" *The Wall Street Journal*: 1, A4 – via New York Public Library.

Thomas, Lewis. *The Medusa and the Snail*, (New York: Penguin Publishing Group, 1995), Kindle Edition, 23. (Reference: Maria Popova, "In Praise of Being Wrong, Lewis Thomas on the Value of Generative Mistakes," *The Marginalian*, March 3, 2023, https://www.themarginalian.org/2023/03/18/lewis-thomas-mistakes/.

Villette, Michel, and Catherine Vuillermot. "From Predators to Icons, Exposing the Myth of the Business Hero," Translated by George Holoch (New York: Cornell University Press), 2009.

Weiss, David, "Dean Kamen on Education," (quoting William Lidwell, "The Dean of Engineering," *Make: Magazine*. Excerpt taken from: https://davidweiss.blogspot.com/search?q=dean+kamen), Accessed June 16, 2024.

Warren, Rick. *The Purpose Driven Life: What on Earth am I Here for?* (Zondervan, Audible audiobook version), 9 hrs., 38 min.

Watts, Larry. Personal interview with the authors. September 1, 2022, and November 10, 2022

Wiseman, Liz. Live speech by Liz Wizeman at RootsTech 2017 reported in article "*Rookie Smarts*," (Evalogue.Life, https://evalogue.life/news-articles/rookie/), accessed June 7, 2024.

Wiseman, Liz. *Rookie Smarts, Enhanced Edition*, (New York: HarperCollins), 100-101, Kindle Edition.

ABOUT THE AUTHORS

James M. Sweeney is a serial entrepreneur who started fourteen healthcare companies, including industry leader Caremark. He has raised two billion dollars in capital, generated more than thirty billion dollars in exit value, and his companies have saved or extended the lives of millions. Today he mentors young entrepreneurs and engages in humanitarian work. He received the Ernst & Young Entrepreneur of the Year award, served on the Harvard Medical School Advisory Board, and received the Lifetime Achievement Award from the Corporate Directors Forum. His alma matter, San Diego State, selected him as Alumnus of the Year in 1986.

Rhonda Lauritzen is a professional biographer and in-demand speaker at international conferences. She has an MBA in entrepreneurship from the University of Utah and has served a stint as CEO of her family's third-generation company, Mineral Resources International. She was a college vice president for ten years. She is the founder of Evalogue.Life where she tells people's stories and teaches others how to tell theirs.